Dear April

As he has touched you, touch others
As he has healed you, heal others.
As he has loved you, love others
As he has taught you, teach others
As he is, as you are becoming, you
are called to help others become.

May God continue to
bless, touch, heal, love, teach
&
call you.

I am grateful to be in <u>his</u>
glorious service with you.

Randy

Aug 06

THE HEALER'S ART

THE HEALER'S ART

Faith and the Healing Power
of Jesus Christ

LLOYD D. NEWELL *and* DON H. STAHELI

DESERET
BOOK

SALT LAKE CITY, UTAH

Library of Congress Cataloging-in-Publication Data

Newell, Lloyd D., 1956–
  The healer's art : faith and the healing power of Jesus Christ/ Lloyd D. Newell and Don H. Staheli.
      p. cm.
  Includes bibliographical references.
  ISBN-10 1-59038-620-5 (hardbound : alk. paper)
  ISBN-13 978-1-59038-620-0 (hardbound : alk. paper)
  1. Spiritual healing—Christianity. 2. Bloch, Carl Heinrich, 1834–1890.
3. Church of Jesus Christ of Latter-day Saints—Doctrines. 4. Mormon Church—Doctrines.
I. Staheli, Don H. II. Title.
  BT732.5.S725 2006
  234'.131—dc22   2006011334

Printed in the United States of America
Publishers Printing, Salt Lake City, UT

10   9   8   7   6   5   4   3   2   1

———•———

To our wives, Karmel Newell and Cyndy Staheli,
whose faith in and practice of the Healer's Art
have been such a blessing

———•———

Table of Contents

TABLE OF CONTENTS

Acknowledgments

It is with sincere gratitude that we recognize the vital contributions of those who have enabled this project to come to fruition. We acknowledge and thank Sheri Dew, Jana Erickson, Richard Peterson, Sheryl Smith, and Laurie Cook at Deseret Book for their encouragement, enthusiasm, and professional expertise; Jack and Mary Lois Wheatley and the staff (particularly Dawn Pheysey) at the Brigham Young University Museum of Art for their generosity, vision, vast knowledge, and wonderful support; Ted Barnes for his willing and helpful assistance with the manuscript; the late Henri J. M. Nouwen, author of *The Return of the Prodigal Son,* for the conceptual inspiration for this project; and our wives, families, and friends who help and heal so much. We feel grateful for artist Carl Bloch whose images inspire us and touch our hearts. And most especially, we reverently offer thanks to the Savior, the Master Healer, from whom all good things flow.

Foreword

Long before Jehovah was born in the flesh, His healing influence was found upon the earth among the faithful people of the Old Testament and the Book of Mormon. Accounts of the Savior's compassionate healings of body, mind, and spirit during His mortal ministry fill the pages of the four gospels, offering hope to all who suffer. Through His priesthood, Christ's disciples continued to bless and heal the afflicted. Journal entries from early members of the restored Church testify of miraculous healings. Modern-day reports of the wondrous restoration of physical, mental, and spiritual health through priesthood blessings are familiar occurrences throughout the world. These accounts stand as sentinels of hope for the afflicted and their loved ones.

However, there are also many instances of those who, in the Lord's own wisdom, are not cured of the effects of illness, accident, or age. Although we acknowledge the infinite understanding and wisdom of the Lord, we sometimes can't refrain from asking the question, "Why me? Why my child? My spouse? Or my friend?"

This past year I attended an inordinate number of funerals for family members and friends. At each of these funerals my testimony of the tender mercies of the Lord and His healing powers was reinforced. But the words spoken at the funeral of a twenty-four-year-old woman who died of cancer remain etched in my mind. The young woman's lifelong friend, reflecting on the things they had learned together, expressed this thought: "You can be cured without being healed, and you can be healed without being cured." As I contemplated the meaning of that profound observation, I began to realize that "healing" embodies something more and something different than merely "curing."

The real miracle of healing begins with knowing and trusting in our Heavenly Father and His Son, Jesus Christ, and willingly submitting to Their will. True healing is always accompanied by a sweet affirmation of comfort and peace "which passeth all understanding" (Philippians 4:7). The Lord has promised us, "I will not leave you comfortless: I will come to you" (John 14:18).

In *The Healer's Art,* authors Lloyd D. Newell and Don H. Staheli present a beautiful and sensitive discourse on healing, in all its varieties. Using the magnificent altarpiece *Christ Healing the Sick at Bethesda,* by Danish artist Carl Heinrich Bloch as a basis for their discussion, these writers explore the miracle of divine healing.

The journey of the *Bethesda* painting to the Brigham Young University Museum of Art is in itself an inspiring confirmation of the Lord's hand in all things. This renowned painting was the first of many significant religious acquisitions that would come to grace the walls of the museum.

It was in 1882 that a group of Copenhagen's Lutheran priests commissioned Carl Heinrich Bloch (1834–1890) to create a painting of Christ healing the sick at Bethesda to celebrate the opening of the Bethesda Indre Mission. For more than a century, the monumental painting remained in its original location behind the pulpit in the ceremonial hall of the Indre Mission in Copenhagen.

Then in 2000, Soren Edsberg, an expatriate Dane living in Provo, Utah, approached the Brigham Young University Museum of Art to determine the museum's interest in acquiring this painting should it become available. Naturally, the museum was intrigued with the possibility because of the Church's deep regard for Bloch's religious paintings. But the acquisition of the masterpiece seemed only remotely possible. After all, it was a large painting that had been commissioned specifically for the Indre Mission bearing the name of Bethesda. The altarpiece was the focal point of the hall, and generations of Lutherans had come to love this magnificent work. Why would they want to part with it? It had also been painted by one of Denmark's most revered nineteenth-century artists. Would Denmark even allow this wonderful work to leave the country? The likelihood of Brigham Young University being able to acquire the painting seemed highly improbable.

Over the next several months, Edsberg worked with the Museum of Art to facilitate negotiations with the Bethesda Indre Mission. It was determined that the Mission might be interested in selling the painting in order to procure the funds needed to complete extensive renovations of its building. In order to accommodate the mission's growing community outreach programs, the building required an upgraded central heating system, new flooring, and painting, as well as other repairs and improvements. The Mission had raised only half of the 14 million kroner needed for the remodeling. Without additional funds, the work could not continue. The sale of the painting would help in the costs of renovation, but because of its long-standing relationship with the people of Copenhagen, the decision to part with the painting was a difficult one. After months of negotiations, an agreement was finally reached, and the painting was sold to the BYU Museum of Art—a purchase that was made possible by the generous donation of Jack and Mary Lois Wheatley, longtime supporters of the museum.

In order for the painting to leave Denmark, permission had to be granted by the Danish government. The Danish Ministry of Cultural Affairs and its Cultural Committee maintain a list of artists whose works are not allowed to leave the country of Denmark because of their classification as national treasures. Surprisingly, in spite of Bloch's prominence during his lifetime and his numerous altarpieces in Denmark and Sweden, as well as his twenty-three paintings on the life of Christ on display at the Frederiksborg Castle, his name inexplicably did not appear on that list. Approval was granted for the sale of the painting.

After contracts were signed, the museum's senior registrar, Susan Thompson, traveled to Denmark to oversee the removal, packing, crating, and shipping of the painting to the United States. The painting arrived at the Museum of Art on the morning of September 10, 2001, one day before the terrorist attacks on the World Trade Center and the Pentagon.

Following the painting's arrival at the Museum of Art, several unveilings were held to announce and celebrate the acquisition. During his BYU Devotional address on September 18, 2001, Elder Merrill J. Bateman, then serving as president of Brigham Young University, encouraged all students, faculty, and staff to visit the Museum of Art to study this masterpiece. In light of the terrorist activities of the previous week, he proffered the painting as a message of hope and healing when he said:

> Christ's healing power is more than physical. He has the power to make a person whole, to heal the soul as well as the body. The magnificent painting by Carl Heinrich Bloch of *Christ Healing the Sick at the Pool of Bethesda* portrays Christ both as a healer and a comforter. The original painting, a wonderful gift . . . will be the signature piece for the Museum

of Art. We hope it will be a constant reminder of our heritage and our mission.

Standing as a witness of the Savior's healing power, this marvelous painting exudes peace and comfort to those who contemplate its profound message. This foreword would not be complete without noting the emotive responses of our museum visitors. According to museum educator Herman du Toit:

> [The painting] has become a source of inspiration and a solace to many. At various times of the day or on evenings when the museum is open, visitors can often be seen in front of this arresting painting. They come as couples, in family groups, or tour parties, but it is often to those who come quietly on their own, when the museum is hushed and a serene air of calmness settles on the gallery, that the irenic power of this salient work is manifest. It is on these occasions that the tender narrative and the healing message of Bloch's work finds place in a yearning or injured heart, when a troubled or anxious spirit is stilled, or despondence dispelled with new hope and affirmation. It is then that quiet resolutions are made, or a difficult decision confirmed, and the power of the Lord's healing Spirit touches one of His children.

Dawn C. Pheysey
Curator of Religious Art
Brigham Young University Museum of Art

Now there is at Jerusalem by the sheep market a pool, which is called in the Hebrew tongue Bethesda, having five porches.

In these lay a great multitude of impotent folk, of blind, halt, withered, waiting for the moving of the water.

For an angel went down at a certain season into the pool, and troubled the water: whosoever then first after the troubling of the water stepped in was made whole of whatsoever disease he had.

And a certain man was there, which had an infirmity thirty and eight years.

When Jesus saw him lie, and knew that he had been now a long time in that case, he saith unto him, Wilt thou be made whole?

The impotent man answered him, Sir, I have no man, when the water is troubled, to put me into the pool: but while I am coming, another steppeth down before me.

Jesus saith unto him, Rise, take up thy bed, and walk.

And immediately the man was made whole, and took up his bed, and walked: and on the same day was the sabbath.

JOHN 5:2–9

Carl Heinrich Bloch
Christ Healing the Sick at Bethesda

CHAPTER ONE

Jesus Christ, the Master Healer

As Jesus Christ performed His mortal ministry, He could be found most often in places where the people were wont to gather—at a wedding feast, in the synagogues, at the temple. He made Himself accessible to all, even those who were usually shunned. His was not a ministry of contemplative isolation but one that placed Him in near-constant contact with people in their daily struggles with life's demands. With equal grace He mingled with the most common folk, tenderly accepted the approach of little children, and received the often hostile advances of the rich and powerful.

In reaching out to those He encountered on the way, Jesus taught and testified, forewarned and forgave, preached and prophesied, declared His divine mission and decried the evils of the day. He cleansed the temple block and fed the hungry. He frustrated and condemned the self-righteous. He praised the meek and poor in spirit. He refused the tempter's snare and calmly, quietly eluded the blood-thirsty rabble who would have stoned Him for telling the truth. In these and myriad other ways He manifested Himself as the Messiah, the Son of God, the Only Begotten of the Father.

But perhaps in no way prior to Gethsemane was His compassion for people revealed more fully than in His miraculous healings. Almost from the beginning, the Lord's public ministry was characterized by the healing of diverse ailments. His fame spread throughout Galilee as a result of this compassionate demonstration of Godly power.

What scenes could be more tender than those of a pleading leper, a beseeching centurion, or a desperate parent, each in need of a healing miracle. They turned with faith to the One who could grant their heartfelt desire; and He, in His limitless love and infinite wisdom, exercised the divine prerogative, and health and wholeness were restored.

Of all the miracles of Jesus recorded in the New Testament, three-fourths of them are described as healings.[1] With all the affectionate sympathy of a devoted parent (for their spiritual Father He was), and with perfect confidence in the height and depth of His power, His heart was drawn out over and over again to bring the joy of health and wholeness to many of the sickly lambs of Judea's fold. Even with His knowledge of the schooling that comes through suffering, He sought to ease the pains of the innocent. In His infinite mercy, He righted the apparent wrongs of nature, smoothed festered flesh, cooled the fevered brow, bade the parting spirit to return, and restored the deceased to the arms of sorrowing loved ones. That He should have been able to do so should be of little wonder. As President Boyd K. Packer has so aptly observed, "Christ is the Creator, the Healer. What He made, He can fix."[2]

Imagine the impact such healings must have had on the mind of the average person living in the Holy Land at the meridian of time. In circumstances where medical treatments were rudimentary at best and probably based as much on superstition and tradition as on science, here came a Man who, with a word or a touch or the application of a little spittle and dirt, healed the most intractable illnesses, corrected lifelong disabilities, and brought back to warm animation those given up for dead.

THE MIRACLE AT THE POOL

One such marvelous incident is recorded by John in the fifth chapter of his Gospel. It occurred at the time of a feast of the Jews, probably the Passover, and Jesus had come up to Jerusalem to celebrate this sacred occasion in memory of God's grace in liberating the children of Israel from the Egyptians. It was a Sabbath day, and Jesus, apparently on His way to the temple, passed near the sheep market by a pool called Bethesda, or House of Mercy.

Surrounding the pool was a "great multitude of impotent folk, of blind, halt, withered" all waiting for a chance to descend into the pool. Tradition held and experience must have given some substance to the belief that when the waters were "troubled" it was the work of an angel, and the first to enter the water thereafter would be healed. Whatever caused the "moving of the water," the healing of those who got to the pool first could only be attributed to their faith in the Divine. One man, lame for thirty-eight years, had not the physical strength to match his great faith, so he lay by the pool in frustration that he was never first to enter the water.

As Jesus passed by the pool of Bethesda, He took notice of the man and by observation or by intuition "knew that he had been a long time in that case." The Master Healer spoke to the impotent man and asked of him, "Wilt thou be made whole?" In deep humility and with no apparent notion of the power of his interrogator, the man addressed the Lord and attempted to explain his plight, "Sir, I have no man . . . to put me into the pool." Said Jesus, "Rise, take up thy bed, and walk." At that instant the lame man was made whole.

There was no need for moving waters or a contest to share the pool with an angel, just a flash of faith and a willingness to follow the command of the Son of God. Such feelings were found in the heart of the unnamed lame man, and nearly four decades of disability were overcome. He was healed! He could walk! He took up his bed and went to the vicinity of the temple, rejoicing in his healing. Perhaps the man, now walking with confidence, went to those sacred precincts with the intent of expressing his gratitude to the God of Israel. Little did he know that it was Israel's God, now on the earth, with whom he had conversed, that it was Jehovah to whom he owed his healing.

New World Healings

One of the remarkable things about the Book of Mormon is that it testifies of a completely Christian people who lived centuries before the actual coming of the Savior. Very early in his revelatory experience, Nephi saw in vision the Lord come to earth to minister to the children of men. He beheld in a vision of the Holy Land "multitudes of people who were sick, and who were afflicted with all manner of diseases, and with devils and unclean spirits. . . . And they were

> *I am the Lord that*
>
> *healeth thee.*
>
> —Exodus 15:26

healed by the power of the Lamb of God; and the devils and the unclean spirits were cast out" (1 Nephi 11:31). Thus, the Nephites, and through them the Lamanites, learned to think of their Savior as Master Healer.

Some 124 years before the Lord was born to Mary, King Benjamin saw Him in anticipatory vision "working mighty miracles, such as healing the sick, raising the dead, causing the lame to walk, the blind to receive their sight, and the deaf to hear, and curing all manner of diseases" (Mosiah 3:5). The early Nephites knew of Jesus Christ and placed their faith in Him with as much trust and confidence as any modern Christians.

And they were healed by the

power of the Lamb of God.

—1 Nephi 11:31

In the Book of Mormon—as in the Old Testament, where Jesus was worshiped as Jehovah—there are powerful examples of the healing power of the Savior long before He came to the earth in the flesh. Those who accepted Him saw no need to await His physical manifestation before they sought to avail themselves of His ability to make them whole.

As Alma the Younger lay on his bed of repentance, his mind caught hold of the teachings of his father, and he invoked the name of Jesus to relieve his suffering. In an impassioned cry for relief, said he, "O Jesus, thou Son of God, have mercy on me, who am in the gall of bitterness, and am encircled about by the everlasting chains of death." His invocation worked a miracle of healing: "And now, behold, when I thought this, I could remember my pains no more" (Alma 36:18–19). One hundred years before He embarked on His earthly sojurn, the Master healed the heart of this young man of great potential.

This same Alma, now serving as a witness of the coming Redeemer, preached the gospel of Jesus Christ with such conviction that the Spirit brought home the truth of his testimony to the heart of one of the Lord's greatest detractors, Zeezrom the lawyer. Alma himself had once been a zealous opponent of the truth, so he could relate well when he and his companion, Amulek, were called to the bed of physical and spiritual misery in which Zeezrom found himself.

"Now, when [Zeezrom] heard that Alma and Amulek were in the land of Sidom, his heart began to take courage; and he sent a message immediately unto them, desiring them to come unto him.

"And it came to pass that they went immediately, obeying the message which he had sent unto them; and they went in unto the house unto Zeezrom; and they found him upon his bed, sick, being very low with a burning fever; and his mind also was exceedingly sore because of his iniquities; and when he saw them he stretched forth his hand, and besought them that they would heal him.

"And it came to pass that Alma said unto him, taking him by the hand: Believest thou in the power of Christ unto salvation?

"And he answered and said: Yea, I believe all the words that thou hast taught.

"And Alma said: If thou believest in the redemption of Christ thou canst be healed.

"And he said: Yea, I believe according to thy words.

"And then Alma cried unto the Lord, saying: O Lord our God, have mercy on this man, and heal him according to his faith which is in Christ.

"And when Alma had said these words, Zeezrom leaped upon

his feet, and began to walk; and this was done to the great astonishment of all the people" (Alma 15:4–11).

It is interesting that Alma asked Zeezrom whether he believed in "the power of Christ unto salvation," not simply in Christ's power to facilitate a physical healing. It would seem that when we have been taught concerning the redemptive mission of Jesus Christ, as Zeezrom had, our faith in Him must be more complete in order to partake of His healing blessing. This is a principle that Jesus Himself taught when he explained, "For unto whomsoever much is given, of him shall be much required" (Luke 12:48).

In addition, we witness in Zeezrom's case something that is often linked to such miraculous healings: a genuine conversion to the gospel of Jesus Christ. In speaking of this phenomenon, Elder Marion G. Romney said that sometimes there is "a physical healing. Sometimes there is also a healing of the nervous system or of the mind. But always the remittance of sins which attends divine forgiveness heals the spirit. This accounts for the fact that in the scriptures conversion and healing are repeatedly associated."[3]

The notion of Christ as Healer is an important theme of the Book of Mormon. Perhaps no single chapter in that volume is more touching than the seventeenth chapter of Third Nephi. In this tender account of the Savior's visit to the Nephite people on the American continent, some of His "other sheep," the Lord said to those gathered at His feet: "Behold, my bowels are filled with compassion towards you. Have ye any that are sick among you? . . .

Bring them hither and I will heal them . . . for I see that your faith is sufficient that I should heal you" (3 Nephi 17:6–8).

Thus, the name of Jesus Christ was evoked in the New World, as it had been in the Old World, to bring about the healing of those who believed in Him. Whether it was before or after His earthly life made no difference. Jehovah had the power to heal before He was manifest in the flesh as the Christ. Just as His priesthood has no end, it had no beginning. Faith in the redemptive power of the Savior could be applied even in anticipation of His successful mortal mission. The faithful who lived before His coming were not penalized by the timing of their birth. They could believe in Him and be blessed of Him as if He had already wrought the Atonement.

MODERN MIRACLES OF HEALING

The healing miracles Jesus performed as recorded in the scriptures seem just as miraculous to us today. The passage of millennia, the advancements of medical science, and the cynicism of modern skeptics have only enhanced the wonder of His loving touch. He was the Master Healer to all those He blessed during His mortal ministry, and He remains the Master Healer for all who seek Him today. His physical presence may not be on the earth in our day, but His power is.

Even in ancient Judah, not all the healing was done by the Master in person. On occasion, His servants were sent to do in His name the work that they had seen Him do. He "gave them power against unclean spirits, to cast them out, and to heal all manner of sickness and all manner of disease" (Matthew 10:1). That same power, restored to the earth through the very apostles who received it from Jesus, is exercised in our day, and still in His holy name. The history of the modern kingdom of God is rich with accounts of healing under the hands of faithful priesthood holders.

The first miracle of the Prophet Joseph Smith's ministry was associated with healing. In April of 1830, the family of Newel Knight sent for Joseph to come at once to their home, for Newel was suffering from a terrible malady. His face and limbs were contorted, and he was being tossed around the room by a power greater than he could overcome by himself. The Prophet Joseph caught him by the hand and commanded in the name of the Lord that the evil spirit that possessed him should depart. Immediately, Brother Knight was relieved of his tormentor.[4]

The healing power of the priesthood of God was often wonderfully manifest through the Prophet Joseph. In July of 1839, following the trials of Missouri, many of the Saints were living along the swampy banks of the Mississippi River. Joseph, who had been sick himself, was camped in Montrose, Iowa. He arose one morning "unexpectedly refreshed and strengthened. Reflecting upon the pitiable situation of the Saints, he called upon the Lord in prayer. The power of God rested upon Him. He healed everyone in his house and in the dooryard. Then, accompanied by

Sidney Rigdon and members of the Twelve, he went among the sick lying on the bank of the river and in the name of Jesus Christ restored them all to health. According to Wilford Woodruff, after healing everyone on the east side of the river, [Joseph] and his companions crossed to Montrose. The first house he entered was that of Brigham Young, who was ill. They healed him, and he rose and went with them. As they passed the door of Wilford Woodruff's dwelling, Joseph called, 'Brother Woodruff, follow me.' They crossed the public square and entered Elijah Fordham's house. The Prophet walked over to the bed and took the dying man by the hand. Fordham's eyes were glazed; the death rattle was in his throat. He was unconscious. Looking into the dying man's face the Prophet asked: 'Brother Fordham, do you not know me?' There was no reply. Joseph spoke again, 'Elijah, do you not know me?'

"From the lips of Fordham came a faint whisper, 'Yes.'

"'Have you not faith to be healed?' the Prophet asked.

"The answer was a little stronger than before. 'I am afraid it is too late; if you had come sooner, I think I might have been.' He had the appearance of a man waking from the sleep of death. The Prophet demanded, 'Do you believe that Jesus is the Christ?' 'I do brother Joseph.' Then the Prophet of God spoke with a loud voice, 'Elijah, I command you, in the name of Jesus of Nazareth, to arise and be made whole.' Fordham arose from his bed, dressed, and asked for a bowl of bread and milk. After eating, he followed the Prophet into the street."[5]

The Prophet Joseph had tremendous confidence in the healing capacity of priesthood power. He also knew that it is personal faith in that power and the grace of God that effects the healing, not the intelligence or the charisma of the man who holds the priesthood, "lest any man should boast" (Ephesians 2:9). Joseph never took undue credit for the works of the Master that were manifested through him, but as he gained experience and understanding, he did become more creative in the exercise of priesthood authority. The story of that special day of healing continues.

After the healing of Elijah Fordham, the group determined to go to those who were suffering on the other side of the Mississippi River. "While Joseph and his brethren waited for the boat to take them across the river to Commerce [later Nauvoo], a man who lived a few miles west of Montrose asked the Prophet to heal his twin babies who were very sick. Joseph regretted that he could not go with the man but assured him that he would send one of his brethren to heal the sick babies. He turned to Wilford Woodruff and asked him to accompany the man to his house and heal the infants. From his pocket the Prophet drew a silk bandanna. [It was a red bandanna some 24 inches square.] Handing it to Elder Woodruff, he told him to wipe the twins' faces

We believe in the gift

of . . . healing.

ARTICLE OF FAITH 7

with it and they would be healed. Then he added: 'As long as you will keep that handkerchief, it shall remain a league between you and me.' Wilford Woodruff did as he was commanded, and the babies were healed."[6] Joseph followed the psalmist's counsel, "He sent his word, and healed them" (Psalm 107:20).

The journals of modern apostles and prophets record many experiences with miraculous healings, made possible through the power of the Lord. As a missionary in England, Wilford Woodruff enjoyed an outpouring of spiritual gifts and "the sick were healed of their sickness, the lame were made to walk, the blind to see, the dumb to speak."[7] In one instance of many healings recorded by Lorenzo Snow, he anointed a young girl who had already died and blessed her that she would come back to life, "because she had not finished her work here on the earth." She did so and lived to rear a large family.[8]

It is the privilege of today's priesthood holders to administer in the name of Jesus of Nazareth to those in distress in the household of faith. Jesus has declared the validity of authorized work done in his name: "Whether by mine own voice or by the voice of my servants, it is the same" (D&C 1:38). It would also hold true if He had said, "whether by my mine own touch," or "whether by mine own administration or by that of my servants, it is the same." The duly appointed servants of the Lord act literally in His stead.

THE POWER OF THE LORD IS CONVEYED
THROUGH HIS SPIRIT

It is vital for each of us to experience the direct influence of the Lord in our lives. Speaking to His disciples, He gave us this wonderful assurance: "Nevertheless I tell you the truth; It is expedient for you that I go away: for if I go not away, the Comforter will not come unto you; but if I depart, I will send him unto you" (John 16:7). It is through the power of the Holy Ghost, the Spirit of the Lord in the life of each person who is willing to receive Him, that we are comforted and healed of our wounds.

When Joseph F. Smith was a young man serving as a full-time missionary in Hawaii, he was nearly overcome with fear and loneliness. One dark night he had a dream in which the healing power of the Lord was shown to him. Through "that vision, that manifestation and witness," he felt as if he "had been lifted out of a slum, out of a despair, out of the wretched condition that [he] was in."[9] In His tender mercy and through the Holy Spirit, the Lord provided His servant the comfort and courage young Joseph so desperately needed.

When the Spirit of the Lord enters into our lives, it is as though He were there Himself to take our hand or dry

To some it is given to have

faith to be healed.

—DOCTRINE AND COVENANTS 46:19

14

our tears. By His Spirit we will be comforted and can be healed of all manner of afflictions, whether physical, emotional, or spiritual.

One person spoke of a particularly spiritual event in his life. He had been laboring under some difficulty and sought the blessings of the Spirit of the Lord. When that Spirit came into his heart, it brought a calm feeling and soothing relief. Though his circumstances were not immediately changed, he had hope that they might be, and he felt energized to do all he could to make things better. He rejoiced in "the healing peace of that experience."[10]

A young woman who had recently lost her husband in a tragic accident went into the temple, the house of the Lord, hoping to find solace for her grief-torn heart. Her family accompanied her and added to hers their faith in Jesus Christ as the Great Physician. Their fondest hopes were realized when the Spirit of the Lord came upon them. Her father wrote, "To her and to our family it was healing. We will never forget."[11]

EACH HEALING IS UNIQUE

The healing hand of the Master touches each person in a manner suited to the individual in need and according to the personal plan of salvation prepared for each of us even before we came to the earth. Every healing is uniquely suited to answer the divine diagnosis of the particular ailment. There is no set formula or timetable for healing. The Lord comes to us one at a time, when the time is right, and blesses us based upon His perfect love and complete knowledge of our circumstances. The Redeemer personalizes His power, sometimes healing the body, other times the mind, and often both, depending on what He deems best for us. Always, it is done in total love.

In His infinite, atoning sacrifice, the Great Healer has suffered "pains and afflictions and temptations of every kind." This He has done "that he may know according to the flesh how to succor [that is to help or comfort] his people according to their infirmities." The Atonement makes possible a personal response to each of us, a response growing out of the Lord's tender mercy and making possible the removal of "the pains and sicknesses of his people" (see Alma 7:11–12). He has suffered so that our own pain might be lessened, or at least understood in its eternal perspective. That He should have chosen to endure what He did in our behalf truly ought to be a matter of wonder, especially when we consider His own description of what it cost Him: "Which suffering caused myself, even God, the greatest of all, to tremble because of pain, and to bleed at every pore, and to suffer both body and spirit" (D&C 19:18).

What he experienced in Gethsemane and on the cross caused, in His word, "exquisite" suffering (D&C 19:15) and as a consequence, there is no pain or difficulty that we might experience that He has not already experienced and endured. There is no extremity He has not visited, no sense of desperation He has not felt. Because His experience is intimate in nature and infinite in depth, His ability to heal us is also infinite. For "the Son of Man hath descended below them all" (D&C 122:8). Thus, He can respond to our pleadings with more than just a generalized empathy, but with a genuine understanding of the depth of our suffering.

When Healing Hopes Are Unmet

Sometimes the healing we desire does not come because the one about whom we are concerned is "appointed unto death" (D&C 42:48). Yet even on such occasions we can find personal healing in the promise "that those that die in [Jesus] shall not taste of death, for it shall be sweet unto them" (D&C 42:46). Thus, in time, our grief will melt away in the warmth of our faith in Him who can make sweet even the most bitter of experiences.

In reality, death is a form of healing. All bodily grief and pain is removed in the transition from mortality to the paradise of God, where we shall be in "a state of rest, a state of peace, where [we] shall rest from all [our] troubles and from all care, and sorrow" (Alma 40:12).

Many modern Jewish congregations pray, "May He Who blessed our ancestors, bless and heal the ill."[12] This prayer (and others similar to it) sounds unselfish and focused on the needs of the person who is sick. Lurking behind such entreaties, however, is often a rather self-centered concern about what will happen to us if our loved one is not healed. We fear the burdens we may have to endure if their healing is not realized.

If our prayer is really for the healing blessing of the one who is in distress, then we can set aside, insomuch as possible, our fear of the pain we would feel if our loved one were not relieved of suffering or should even pass away. Our prayer must be offered in an attitude of true submission to the will of the Master Healer, "even as a child doth submit to his father" (Mosiah 3:19).

The Savior will heal according to His divine mind and heart and will. The very suffering from which we pray for relief may ultimately be a healing in disguise. For in our suffering, we can learn and come to special understanding, which might not be achieved through any other means. As the Lord revealed to the Prophet Joseph as he languished in despair in the Liberty Jail, "If the heavens gather blackness, and all the elements combine to hedge up the way; . . . know thou, my son, that all these things shall give thee experience, and shall be for thy good" (D&C 122:7). "And then, if thou endure it well, God shall exalt thee on high; [and] thou shalt triumph" (D&C 121:8).

In tribute to the healing power of the Lord Jesus Christ, artist Carl Bloch created his masterpiece painting of *Christ Healing the Sick at Bethesda.* (See the foreword of this book.) Here is depicted the pure love of Christ, applied without respect to the social or economic status of the recipient. The Lord knows the need of the one in distress and can sense the degree of faith harbored in his heart.

He then wields the powers of heaven in a miraculous manifestation of grace.

This volume is not intended to be a comprehensive study of the gift and doctrine of healing, but is intended to offer observations on the various scenes in Bloch's painting, how these scenes relate to the main thematic element—the healing power of Jesus Christ— and some of the application we might find for our own lives in this wonderful work of art. Our hope is that as you study the painting, consider your personal experience, and listen to the whisperings of the Spirit of the Lord, you may gain greater insight into the Healer's art and its power and meaning in your life.

CHAPTER TWO

The Crowd at the Pool

In Bloch's classic altarpiece, Jesus has entered the vicinity of the sheep market and the community water supply. He stands within a substantial structure with walls of stone and massive supporting pillars. It seems to be a place of much traffic and the bustle of commerce. Being an animal market, it was certainly subject to the typical pollutions, the sounds and odors, of such a place. Yet with everything going on that would rob the setting of purity and peace, there enters the majestic personage of the Messiah, and around Him is an aura of quiet holiness. The marketplace is transformed into a temple for the period of His presence.

The sunlight streaming into the openings in the back wall gives some illumination to the scene. Through these openings, far in the background, we can see the green of springtime in the holy city of

Jerusalem. The sun in the heavens sheds its light on the city while the Son of Man spreads abroad the light of truth.

THE DISTRACTIONS OF THE WORLD

In the painting, the Savior stands with His back to the milling crowd. Directly behind Him is a personage thought to represent Peter, who seems to be striking a protective pose, as if to keep the crowd from thronging the Master and disrupting this moment of His ministry. It appears as though Peter might sense the need to move the Lord along, so to avoid a potentially insecure situation. Regardless of his intention, the Peter figure seems to be giving the Lord less credit than He deserves in managing the task at hand. Peter may be thinking the Savior is unaware of something that Peter must bring to His attention. In reality, the Master Healer is completely in control and is about to exercise His power in behalf of one man, with little heed to the noise and hubbub of the world around Him.

In the painting, Christ pays no attention to the bustling group. It is as though they represent the distractions of the world, and He has more meaningful work to do. He is fully focused on the lame man and is determined to let His word alight upon the one in need, like a dove with healing in its wings.

The motives of the men in the background are not obvious, but the stance of the Peter figure does not seem to indicate that they are friends. Only one or two appear to notice the Savior at all. We could assume that they are unaware of what is happening before them. Perhaps they are preoccupied with the tasks of the day, too busy to realize that the key to their eternal life is standing right next to them and that a miracle is about to occur. The men of the market are oblivious to the fact that within their grasp is the One who has been sent to the earth to redeem them from the bonds of earthly frustration and chaos. All of the fear and concern of their lives could be wiped away in the peace of His Spirit, if they only knew how to apply its healing balm.

The onlookers in the painting, and too often all of us, yield to the importuning of the world and thoughtlessly join the mass of humanity as it is pulled along by impulse and the momentum of the moment. We run so fast from task to task, from pillar to post in the barren sheep markets of the world, trying desperately to find our way, to fit in, and to feel good. Yet we often fail to grant the most important things of life the attention they deserve, to give notice to the healing touch of the Savior of mankind and to the restorative beauty of His glorious creations. We do not lift our eyes to see what really matters, to pause and allow time for the true joys of life to distill upon our souls.

The Lord will not manifest Himself to those who give Him no regard. He does not force Himself upon us or demand our consideration. His voice comes not with the roar of a mighty wind nor the rumbling of an earthquake, but like a whisper in the night, sometimes so quietly we can hardly hear it. While the rest of the crowd works on in mindless acts of material acquisition, we can listen to the promptings of the Spirit. We can give it the full attention of our mind and heart. We can hear, and the message will be clear. Then we can arise, take up our bed, and walk in the direction deemed best for us by a loving Lord and Savior.

Bloch placed additional figures to the right of the center pillar. One of them appears to be disabled in some manner, as he is standing with the help of a crutch. Those in front of and behind the man with the crutch do not look physically handicapped. They all seem, however, to be kept from seeing the works of the Master by a thick wall of preoccupation with the things of the world. Like a barrier of earthly cares, the pillar stands between them and the source of their salvation. They do not know what is taking place so nearby and yet so far from the realm of their awareness.

The Prophet Joseph Smith spoke of his vision of the Twelve in very difficult circumstances: "I saw the Twelve Apostles of the Lamb, who are now upon the earth, who hold the keys of this last ministry, in foreign lands, standing together in a circle, much fatigued, with their clothes tattered and feet swollen, with their eyes cast downward, and Jesus standing in their midst, and they did not behold Him. The Savior looked upon them and wept."[13]

Sometimes our tiredness and hopelessness can cause us to become overly concerned with what is going on around us and to hang our heads in despair. If we can lift our eyes in faith, we might feel the Spirit of comfort and relief. Even when our lives are tattered and torn, we can rest assured that the Savior looks upon us in love.

One might be so busy looking for an earthly cure to life's ills that the quiet treatment of the Spirit is overlooked. President Harold B. Lee taught the following to a group of students:

"A few weeks ago, President [David O.] McKay related to the Twelve an interesting experience. . . . He said it is a great thing to be responsive to the whisperings of the Spirit, and we know that when these whisperings come it is a gift and our privilege to have them. They come when we are relaxed and not under pressure. . . . The President then took occasion to relate an experience in the life of Bishop John Wells, former member of the Presiding Bishopric.

"A son of Bishop Wells was killed in Emigration Canyon on a railroad track. Brother John Wells was a great detail man and prepared many of the reports we are following up now. His boy was run over by a freight train. Sister Wells was inconsolable. She mourned during the three days prior to the funeral, received no comfort at the funeral, and was in a rather serious state of mind.

"One day soon after the funeral services while she was lying on her bed relaxed, still mourning, she said her son appeared to her and said, 'Mother, do not mourn, do not cry. I am all right.' He told her that she did not understand how the accident happened and explained that he had given the signal to the engineer to move on, and then made the usual effort to catch the railing on the freight train; but as he attempted to do so his foot caught on a root and he failed to catch the handrail, and his body fell under the train. It was clearly an accident.

"Now, listen. He said that as soon as he realized that he was in another environment he tried to see his father, *but couldn't reach him. His father was so busy with the duties in his office he could not respond to his call.* Therefore he had come to his mother. He said to her, 'You tell Father that all is well with me, and I want you not to mourn anymore.'"[14]

In Bloch's painting, the man with the crutch and those around him seem far too busy with the tasks at hand to notice that very near them is the One who can give whatever comfort they may need. In their day and even now, the Master Healer can answer "Why?" and "How?" and "When?" and "Where?" if we will but listen. His Spirit lingers near to give us the healing comfort that we seek.

THE SAVIOR WILL HEAL *YOU*

Barely visible in the lower left corner of the painting is a sad, shuffling, deformed figure who does seem to be noticing what the Savior is doing. He is likely a witness of this wonderful miracle. There is no record, however, of his beseeching the Master for a similar and most assuredly needed healing blessing. He may represent those who believe in the healing power of the Master, but see no application of it for themselves.

The Book of Mormon prophet Alma made reference to a group of Old Testament people who seem to have taken an approach similar to the crippled man who peers from behind the Master in Bloch's painting. Alma speaks of the children of Israel who followed Moses into the wilderness. In an attempt to humble them, Jehovah sent poisonous serpents to their camp. Some were bitten and died. The Lord did not, however, leave them without recourse should they fall prey to the deadly fangs. He commanded Moses to lift up a symbol of the Master Healer—ironically a brazen serpent— upon which those who were bitten might look and be healed. "And," says Alma, "many did look and live" (Alma 33:19). A substantial number had faith enough to look to the type of their salvation and receive His healing blessing.

Thy faith hath made thee whole.

—MATTHEW 9:22

The news of their healing must have spread like wildfire through the camp of Israel. Everyone would have learned of the brazen serpent and of the healing of those who gazed upon it in faith. Why, then, would not each one who was poisoned rush to the standard and look with hope upon the emblem fashioned by the prophet for their healing? Alma explains that it was not because they did not believe that doing so would result in healing. There was already plenty of evidence that the healing would occur and had occurred for many people. "But there were many who were so hardened that they would not look, therefore they perished. Now the reason they would not look is because they did not believe that it would heal them" (Alma 33:20).

Be sure to place the emphasis on the final word of that sentence. "They did not believe that it would heal *them*." They knew it would heal, for many had been so blessed, but they had become so hardened, so cynical, so hopeless, so faithless regarding their own lives that they did not believe that it would heal *them*.

Many even in our day have a testimony of the Atonement, of the healing power of the Master, but believe that these things apply only in the lives of others, not in their own. They can bear witness to the grace of the Redeemer but cannot bring themselves to really believe it can be applied to such as they. Thus, they fail to look and perish in their hardness and hopelessness.

The deformed man, forced to move about using his hands as feet, may have been hardened by his life of crawling and begging. He was subjected to the pity, the disdain, or even worse, the complete disregard of those who towered over him and whose dust he ate as they walked by carrying goods from the market. He may have become so doubtful of the kindness of others that he could not appreciate the divine manifestation of pure love being displayed before his very eyes. To him it may have been just one more favor that would be withheld from a person of his most lowly position.

Though in the painting he sees the healing power, he does not believe that it can heal *him*.

We must avoid feelings of such skepticism and hopelessness regarding our own standing in the heart and mind of the Master Healer. We are never too far beneath Him to seek His blessing. He does not qualify His love, though it has been quantified and found in ample supply, even enough to fill all eternity.

SMALL AND SIMPLE THINGS

Another barrier to healing is the notion that some grand and monumental event must occur in the process or that the administration of healing priesthood power must come under the hand and authority of a man of high position. It is often the quiet and simple things, actions that may seem too easy, carried out by the regular people with whom we are so familiar, that have the greatest impact—worthy fathers, brothers, home teachers, and bishops, men who know and love us, hold the same priesthood, and can apply its power as well as anyone.

I have seen thy tears:

behold, I will heal thee.

—2 KINGS 20:5

Remember the story of Naaman who figured he had to see the prophet Elisha himself and have an extra-special experience in order to be healed of his leprosy. Elisha and Naaman's good servants helped him to humble himself and learn the truth:

29

"So Naaman came with his horses and with his chariot, and stood at the door of the house of Elisha.

"And Elisha sent a messenger unto him, saying, Go and wash in Jordan seven times, and thy flesh shall come again to thee, and thou shalt be clean.

"But Naaman was wroth, and went away, and said, Behold, I thought, He will surely come out to me, and stand, and call on the name of the Lord his God, and strike his hand over the place, and recover the leper.

"Are not Abana and Pharpar, rivers of Damascus, better than all the waters of Israel? may I not wash in them, and be clean? So he turned and went away in a rage.

"And his servants came near, and spake unto him, and said, My father, if the prophet had bid thee do some great thing, wouldest thou not have done it? how much rather then, when he saith to thee, Wash, and be clean?

"Then went he down, and dipped himself seven times in Jordan, according to the saying of the man of God: and his flesh came again like unto the flesh of a little child, and he was clean" (2 Kings 5:9–14).

Trying to help his son Helaman understand this principle, Alma taught the young man: "Now ye may suppose that this is foolishness in me; but behold I say unto you, that by small and simple things are great things brought to pass; and small means in many instances doth confound the wise" (Alma 37:6). Helaman learned this lesson well and later took some two thousand boys—simple, faithful children of the Ammonites—into battle against the hardened and powerful Lamanite army—and won (see Alma 56).

The Lord restored His Church through a simple farm boy. In our day, the vast majority of the full-time missionaries are still in their teens or early twenties. The Savior often sends His message to the world through youth. The Master Healer is truly a master at using the strength of those who appear to be weak.

If we would be healed of our illness or distress, we need not look for the grandiose cure, the burning bush, the rushing wind. Fireworks and celebrities are not the way of the Lord. Simple faith, plain prayer, and the administration of a humble priesthood bearer can bring to pass great things.

There went virtue out of him, and healed them all.

—LUKE 6:19

CHAPTER THREE

The Man in the Red Cap

There is a balm in Gilead
To make the wounded whole
There is a balm in Gilead
To heal the sin-sick soul.

Sometimes I feel discouraged,
And think my work's in vain,
But then the Holy Spirit,
Revives my soul again,

If you cannot preach like Peter,
If you cannot pray like Paul,
You can tell the love of Jesus,
And say, "He died for all."

Don't ever feel discouraged,
For Jesus is your friend,

And if you lack of knowledge
He'll ne'er refuse to lend.

There is a balm in Gilead
To make the wounded whole
There is a balm in Gilead
To heal the sin-sick soul.[15]

Crouched against a sturdy stone pillar in Bloch's painting is a weakened man whose leg is wrapped in an soiled bandage. His red cap and wary eyes draw us to him. Indeed, we might have a disquieting sense that something about him is found in each of us.

Except for his red cap, he is bereft of worldly possessions. His ragged robe is too large for his emaciated body, as if to suggest that he was once more robust. Now he is weaker, thinner, more tired. His wounded leg is but a manifestation of a wounded spirit as he looks distrustful, even resentful. The whiskers on his face catch the sunlight; he appears unkempt and older than his years—both in body and in spirit. The tight grip the man holds around his legs suggests a spirit not fully ready to submit. It appears that he still wants to control and even protect his injury rather than turn it over to the Savior.

The red cap on his head may be a proud remnant of a former life and accomplishments, even a signal to others that he was once a person of station. Aside from the Savior's resplendent white robe, the man's red cap is the brightest thing in the painting. Our eyes go from Christ's healing encounter to the eyes of the man in the red cap. As circumspect as the man may seem, he is turned slightly toward the Savior. The focus of his eyes signifies an interest in the Savior's healing power, as if to say, though reluctantly, "Is there healing for me as well?"

Love is the balm that

brings healing to the soul.

—THOMAS S. MONSON

We are drawn to his dark, deliberate eyes. They indicate that he *feels* something before he sees anything. His eyes meet our eyes in his questioning, as if to acknowledge that we are not just observers in this story. In a sense, we too have come to the pool to be healed. But we may also be on his side of the pillar—afraid, hesitant, yet wanting to be healed.

Of all the people we see in *Christ Healing the Sick at Bethesda,* the man in the red cap most demands our attention. Everyone in the painting has a story to tell, but we want to know this man's story most of all. Who is he? What has happened in his life? Will he too be healed? Perhaps this man is so intriguing because we see our own pains and heartaches in him. Who has not felt wounded or broken and wondered if healing could be found? Who has not held onto some bitterness, fearful of being hurt or disappointed again?

No one gets through life without needing help and healing. We

I cried unto thee, and

thou hast healed me.

—PSALM 30:2

pray and hope and continue to believe that "earth has no sorrow that heav'n cannot heal."[16] President Thomas S. Monson has said: "At times there appears to be no light at the tunnel's end—no dawn to break the night's darkness. We feel surrounded by the pain of broken hearts, the disappointment of shattered dreams, and the despair of vanished hopes. We join in uttering the biblical plea, 'Is there no balm in Gilead?' (Jeremiah 8:22). We are inclined to view our own personal misfortunes through the distorted prism of pessimism. We feel abandoned, heartbroken, alone. To all who so despair, may I offer the assurance of the Psalmist's words: 'Weeping may endure for a night, but joy cometh in the morning' (Psalm 30:5)."[17] The healing balm of Gilead is available to each of us.

Perhaps the man in the red cap has heard of such a balm. Maybe he's been told of a healer come from God, "teaching in [the] synagogues, and preaching the gospel of the kingdom, and healing all manner of sickness and all manner of disease among the people" (Matthew 4:23). Perhaps he now wonders, "Is it true? Could it be He?"

The man in the red cap, though

Art to be art must soothe.

—MOHANDAS GHANDI

half-hearted and wary, is not a lost soul. He may still be bound by some anger, but he does turn toward healing. Maybe dashed hopes and previous disillusionments have made him more cautious, distrustful, even reluctant to fully embrace the light he now begins to sense. Perhaps arrogance has gotten the best of him: the pride that led him to his spiritually wounded condition, the pride that keeps him from being healed. But he has not completely given up or given in to pride. Faith has brought him to the pool, and there he sits, perhaps daily, wondering, watching, waiting.

We too wonder at times if we'll ever be well again. Sometimes it's as if we're standing at water's edge, believing to a degree but lacking the faith to wholly embrace what our heart knows is true. We wait and watch for healing, for peace, for some relief from the pains and trials of life.

PAIN PRECEDES HEALING

Each of us who has lived for any length of time has discovered that heartbreak, illness, and emotional or spiritual distress are part of life. At times these adversities impact us and the people we love so severely that they consume our every thought and motion, sometimes briefly and other times for years on end. Sometimes we even feel defined by our maladies—or those of the people we love: we become a man with a withered hand, a woman who has been suffering hemorrhages for twelve years, or a woman whose daughter has an unclean spirit (see Mark 3:1; 5:25; 7:25). We long for the healing touch of the Master's hand—for the gentle touch that will make us whole—or we yearn to be able to offer this touch of wholeness to someone we love.

Dennis and Michelle have known something about heartache. They married as college students with a world of hope and possibility before them. Blessed with five children, a gratifying job as a teacher, and fulfilling opportunities to serve in the Church, they felt content and that things were going well for them. Then, as it does for so many of us, life took an unexpected turn. David started experiencing severe headaches. He had no energy; his vision began to blur. In time, he was diagnosed with an inoperable brain tumor. Several months later, he was dead, and Michelle was left alone with her five children, dashed hopes, and an uncertain future. She came face to face with questions of faith: Is there truly a God? Can I believe Him? Do I trust Him? When the pain is so deep and the heartache unbearable, is healing possible? After asking the hard questions but remaining soft enough to receive answers, Michelle can attest that healing *is* possible, but she will admit that it is painful.

Sometimes, especially at first, it may seem less painful to avoid healing—to proudly deny the pain. Ultimately, however, denial gives rise to other and usually more serious maladies than sorrow or loss.

A physician who has spent much of her medical career counseling the chronically and terminally ill, Rachel Naomi Remen has learned that acknowledging pain is a prerequisite for healing: "Many of us repress our losses and carry our own pain ungrieved, often for years. We have become numb, not because we don't care but because we don't grieve. Grief is the way that loss heals."[18] In other words, we have to go *through* the pain, not *around* it, in order to feel whole again.

Just as a physician has to treat the source of pain in order for the symptoms to go away, we must be willing to undergo the full spiritual and emotional treatment to heal from spiritual and emotional maladies. Jesus' healing power can purge festering wounds, even cure chronic problems, but we must be willing to do whatever the Lord requires. For example, when Christ healed the man who had been blind from birth, He first spat into the dirt, made some clay, and anointed the man's eyes. The blind man did not question the unconventional treatment. Rather, with a grateful heart,

> *Jesus . . . said unto him, Dost thou believe on the Son of God? . . . And he said, Lord, I believe.*
>
> —JOHN 9:35, 38

he accepted the Savior's treatment and further demonstrated his faithfulness by washing in the pool of Siloam—just as the Savior had instructed. The man was submissive, teachable, and believing. He was willing to do *all* that he was asked, and therefore he was healed (see John 9:1–7).

What C. S. Lewis said so well about becoming perfect we can apply to becoming healed: "Once you call [Christ] in, He will give you the full treatment.

"That is why He warned people to 'count the cost' before becoming Christians. 'Make no mistake,' He says, 'if you let me, I will make you perfect. The moment you put yourself in My hands, that is what you are in for. Nothing less, or other, than that. You have free will, and if you choose, you can push Me away. But if you do not push Me away, understand that I am going to see this job through. Whatever suffering it may cost you . . . , whatever it costs Me, I will never rest, nor let you rest, until you are literally perfect—until my Father can say without reservation that He is well pleased with you, as He said He was well pleased with me. This I can do and will do. But I will not do anything less.'"[19] Indeed, as the apostle Paul said, we do all things—including becoming healed—through Jesus Christ (see Philippians 4:13).

> *Return unto thy rest,*
>
> *O my soul; for the Lord*
>
> *hath dealt bountifully*
>
> *with thee.*
>
> —PSALM 116:7

LETTING GO OF PRIDE

We cannot be healed until we let go of personal pride and come unto the Savior. We have to be willing to submit to the Master Healer. No matter the loneliness, sorrow, difficulty or distress, we can find rest to our souls, but only if we submit our will and sincerely offer, "Not as I will, but as thou wilt" (Matthew 26:39). Sometimes we cling so tightly to the vestiges of our independence, like the man in Bloch's painting who insists on wearing his red cap with his rags, that we prevent our own healing. The trials that should humble us instead merely make us ashamed of our dependence and, ironically, less willing to submit to healing. Pride exacerbates our spiritual injuries and perceived grievances, and none of us is entirely immune from its infection. President Ezra Taft Benson taught: "Pride affects all of us at various times and in various degrees. Now you can see why the building in Lehi's dream that represents the pride of the world was large and spacious and great was the multitude that did enter into it. (See 1 Ne. 8:26, 33; 11:35–36.) Pride is the universal sin, the great vice."[20]

The scriptures are filled with antidotes for pride or positive steps we can take to counteract and even prevent pride from entering our hearts. These antidotes are, in effect, healing agents. In fact, the gospel of Jesus Christ is a comprehensive plan for wellness. Christ is the Master Healer. And His gospel *is* healing. Among the healing agents that the scriptures repeatedly emphasize are forgiveness, humility, knowledge, and charity.

FORGIVENESS

Forgiveness is perhaps the most potent soul-medicine available. What greater release from the pains of life can be found than to forgive another? The Lord has commanded us to "forgive one another; for he that forgiveth not his brother his trespasses standeth condemned before the Lord; for there remaineth in him the greater sin" (D&C 64:9). The love of God gives us the desire, and faith in the Atonement gives us the strength to unlock prison doors of bitterness. Sincere and regular prayer helps transform resentful hearts into forgiving hearts and skeptical hearts into believing hearts. If we begin to exercise even a particle of faith, that faith can take root, flourish, and blossom into a harvest of steadfast and immovable confidence in the Lord (see Alma 32).

He healeth the

broken in heart.

—PSALM 147:3

We begin by refusing to retaliate. The Savior taught, "Whosoever shall smite thee on thy right cheek, turn to him the other also. . . . And whosoever shall compel thee to go a mile, go with him twain" (Matthew 5:38–41). Concerning this teaching of the Master, President Gordon B. Hinckley said: "The application of this principle, difficult to live but wondrous in its curative powers, would have a miraculous effect on our troubled homes. It is selfishness which is the cause of most of our misery. It is as a cankering disease. The healing power of Christ, found in the doctrine of going the second mile, would do wonders to still argument and accusation, fault-finding and evil speaking."[21] Pride engenders bitterness, discord, and recrimination; in other words, pride keeps us from forgiving and, thereby, from being healed.

HUMILITY

Humility invites healing. Humility is recognizing that we are dependent upon God's grace and that we not only can but *must* ask for divine help. Those who are humble remember that "the worth of souls is great in the sight of God" (D&C 18:10). They understand that we are sons and daughters of God and, as such, seek to lay claim on His mercy and blessings. Humility is the opposite of enmity; it is to be meek and teachable and, with an honest heart, strive to do good works.

"The Lord requireth the heart and a willing mind" (D&C 64:34). The essence of what the Lord requires of us is living the gospel with a humble heart. In fact, having "a broken heart and a contrite spirit" sets the healing process in motion: "Ye shall offer for a sacrifice unto me a broken heart and a contrite spirit. And whoso cometh unto me with a broken heart and a contrite spirit, him will I baptize with fire and with the Holy Ghost" (3 Nephi 9:20). A broken heart is open to receive wisdom, love, and divine guidance. A broken heart seeks for divine succor from Him who "healeth the broken in heart, and bindeth up their wounds" (Psalm 147:3). If we can hold on to the humility we feel in the midst of a trial, we can find healing, growth, and newness of life.

KNOWLEDGE

Another way to find healing is to renounce any crippling false-hoods, myths, lies, or deceptions that may entangle us. As trials come, we must sort truth from error and cling to everlasting things. We must hearken unto the Way, the Truth, and the Life, who instructs us that "all these things shall give thee experience, and shall be for thy good" (D&C 122:7). Living truthfully means that we strive to walk in righteousness and faithfulness; we focus on sincere effort, not competition and comparisons; we strive to have humble and grateful hearts. Living truthfully means that we choose to obey, even if we have questions and don't fully understand all things (see Moses 5:5–7).

In regard to living truthfully, Elder Henry B. Eyring said: "We need strength beyond ourselves to keep the commandments in whatever circumstance life brings to us. For some it may be poverty, but for others it may be prosperity. It may be the ravages of age or the exuberance of youth. The combination of trials and their duration are as varied as are the children of our Heavenly Father. No two are alike. But what is being tested is the same, at all times in our lives and for every person: will we do whatsoever the Lord our God will command us?"[22] Those who meekly know and live the truth are in a position to be healed.

Truth makes us free—free from falsehood and deceit, debilitating doubt and despair (see John 8:32). Truth allows for healing and wholeness. Only by knowing and living truth can we find peace of mind and peace of conscience. Elder Richard G. Scott said: "In these times of increasing uncertainty there is so much heartache, anguish, and suffering throughout the world that could be avoided by understanding and applying truth."[23] The truth embodied in Christ and His transcendent teachings gives us the power to be healed.

Peace cannot be bought or bartered or falsely created. We cannot psych ourselves into peace of mind or conscience with a pep talk or motivational mantra. Peace of mind and heart comes from living truthfully, from having integrity, from congruence with true principles. To live according to the foolish whims and wisdom of the world, without the illuminating truths of the restored gospel, is to be forever wary and worried. To seek healing without seeking truth is to wander in darkness when the light of noonday sun is available (see D&C 95:6).

He shall rise from the dead,

with healing in his wings.

2 NEPHI 25:13

CHARITY

Charity is the pure, undefiled love of Christ, which "suffereth long, and is kind; charity envieth not; charity vaunteth not itself, is not puffed up. Doth not behave itself unseemly, seeketh not her own, is not easily provoked, thinketh no evil; Rejoiceth not in iniquity, but rejoiceth in the truth; Beareth all things, believeth all things, hopeth all things, endureth all things. Charity never faileth" (1 Corinthians 13:4–8). This perfect love casts out fear, lifts anger and bitterness, and engenders an understanding and patient heart. That's a good description of what healing feels like.

When the Savior told his twelve apostles that one of them would betray him, they felt sorrowful and began to ask, "Lord, is it I?" (Matthew 26:22). Although good men, they still felt the need to do some soul-searching—and sincerely repent, if necessary. Charity leads us to ask the meek question, "Is it I?" When the answer is yes, repentance helps us to feel again the love of God and, in turn, share that love with others. The more we strive to *be* charitable, the more we are blessed with charity. Charity is indeed the sustaining love of God whose reach is upon all peoples and nations (see 2 Nephi 24:26). Charity both enables healing and becomes healing. To feel charity is to be healed.

BECOME ALIVE IN CHRIST

When a loss shocks our soul or we encounter some sort of trauma, we may feel as if the wind were knocked out of us for a time. In a sense, we suffer a kind of death. We're never quite the same, but we go on. In process of time, the loss we endure makes room for a newness of life. As we are healed and the sorrow fades, we notice again the way a toddler giggles. We are able to listen more intently to a bird's song and a child's prayer. The change of seasons once more comforts us and the beauty of nature inspires us. We are able to appreciate more fully the love and affection of family and friends. The prosaic, simple moments of yesterday and today once more give us hope that life has purpose and meaning beyond the here and now. We again muster the strength to hold on to that hope and wait patiently for some healing peace. We begin to recall details about our life before the trauma, and we cherish anew the memories.

To be healed is to find new life. When the Master Healer extends His arm of mercy and we come unto Him, we are born again into joy and happiness. The gospel teaches us that we are to be alive in Christ and become new creatures in Him (see 2 Nephi 25:25; Mosiah 27:25–26). Becoming alive in Christ begins by acknowledging our brokenness, our need for healing. In other words, becoming alive in Christ begins by shedding our pride. Just as the man in the red cap, we need to own up to our shortcomings and not get stuck protecting them from divine scrutiny. As we examine ourselves truthfully, we'll see areas in our hearts that need improvement, areas in our souls

Lord . . . speak the word only, and my servant shall be healed.

—MATTHEW 8:8

that need meekness. If we can be authentic in our relationship with God, we can begin to see how much He loves us and how willing He is to help us be whole again.

Once we recognize our pride and begin the lifelong effort to overcome it, we realize that we cannot heal ourselves. We need God's help. We must turn to Him with full purpose of heart. When we mourn the loss of a loved one, when hopes vanish or dreams dissolve, when hearts deeply ache, it takes more than willpower to keep going. To truly move forward with our lives we must trust God and know that His great plan of happiness is for *each one of us,* His children. Abiding faith helps us see that life has meaning beyond the present pain. Humble submission to a greater good gives us the unwavering conviction that someday wrongs will be righted.

In the classic novel *Little Women* by Louisa May Alcott, the spirited older sister Jo mourns the untimely death of her younger sister Beth. She consoles herself with these words:

> *My great loss becomes my gain.*
> *For the touch of grief will render*
> *My wild nature more serene,*
> *Give to life new aspirations,*
> *A new trust in the unseen.*[24]

Jo's faith, now tested, carves a depth of character into her soul that was not realized before she lost her sister. She becomes more patient, more disciplined, more motivated to use her talents, more trusting in God's will. Her loss becomes her gain.

The same can be true for us. When we have the courage to believe and the strength to endure, pain and grief can give way to wisdom, spiritual maturity, and a greater capacity to love. Heartache and suffering

The basic source for the healing of the soul is the Atonement of Jesus Christ.

—JAMES E. FAUST

can bestow quiet confidence in divine purposes and a deeper appreciation for life. The apostle Paul taught: "Most gladly therefore will I rather glory in my infirmities, that the power of Christ may rest upon me. Therefore I take pleasure in infirmities, in reproaches, in necessities, in persecutions, in distresses for Christ's sake: for when I am weak, then am I strong" (2 Corinthians 12:9–10).

The more we submit and consecrate, the more our trials and sufferings are "swallowed up in the joy of Christ" (Alma 31:38). The process of spiritual growth can be long and hard—yet it can also be joyful. When we exercise faith in the Lord and seek righteousness, we have hope in the future and power in the present. Victor Hugo advised: "Have courage for the great sorrows of life, and patience for the small ones; and when you have laboriously accomplished your daily task, go to sleep in peace. God is awake."[25]

And his servant was healed

in the selfsame hour.

—MATTHEW 8:13

No matter how tired we may be and how weary our efforts become, God is watching over us. He is our loving Father, our Master Caretaker.

"We must not lose hope. Hope is an anchor to the souls of men," said President Ezra Taft Benson. "Satan would have us cast away that anchor. In this way he can bring discouragement and surrender. But we must not lose hope. The Lord is pleased with every effort, even the tiny, daily ones in which we strive to be more like Him. Though we may see that we have far to go on the road to perfection, we must not give up hope."[26] As we grow spiritually and our faith deepens we can join with Nephi in saying, "I know that he loveth his children; nevertheless, I do not know the meaning of all things" (1 Nephi 11:17). In our sorrow we can nurture the faith to "be still, and know that [He is] God" (Psalm 46:10). We can grasp the iron rod with both hands and hold on to the sweet assurance that He slumbers not nor sleeps as He watches over us with perfect love (see Psalm 121:4). He taught that the poor in spirit, the meek and merciful and those who mourn would be blessed (see Matthew 5:3–10). He promised that He would not leave us comfortless (see John 14:18). The Master Healer spoke of the divine commission He received from His Father: "The Spirit of the Lord is upon me, because he hath anointed me to preach the gospel to the poor; he hath sent me to heal the brokenhearted, to preach deliverance to the captives, and recovering of sight to the blind, to set at liberty them that are bruised" (Luke 4:18). To all who come to the pool of Bethesda, wary and fearful of disappointment, wondering if healing and joy are possible, the Lord's promise is sure: He can heal us.

CHAPTER FOUR

The Women Come for Water

At the far right of the Bloch painting we see what appear to be three generations in familial formation, approaching the pool—mother, child, and grandmother. The mother's protective hand draws the child close to her side. It would seem the child is comfortable there and clings tightly to Mother's side in the crowded and somewhat chaotic market place. Grandmother follows behind. She has yielded the lead to the younger generation and is now content to follow in support of what seems to be a mission to obtain water.

In this interesting threesome, Bloch has provided an intriguing image of some of the primary functions of a family—nurture, protection, and support. Mother is gathering the means for the physical nurturance of the family as she obtains water. She also gives the child a tender caress of love, which is so vital to the child's emotional well-being. The child in the painting looks well fed and well loved.

The mother also offers the child a protecting hand and a skirt for the child to cling to for a secure connection to Mother's physical presence. The child need not fear, as long as there is a tight grip on Mother's robes.

Grandmother guards from the background. She is not as overtly involved in caring for the child but she plays a vital role nonetheless in seeing that the trip to the pool for water is carried out safely. She offers an additional set of eyes to protect the child when the mother focuses on filling the jug. She may also be able to assist in lifting the heavy receptacle to the shoulder of her daughter so it may be carried home. Grandparents can offer a supportive influence that has a profound impact on the ultimate success of even everyday endeavors.

Why such emphasis on a family performing a routine task in a painting about healing? Because there is healing in family routines and rituals. The things we are used to doing, the things we do almost every day or which are part of the tradition in our family celebrations, bring peace and a sense of belonging. Strong families often carry on traditions for multiple generations. Each new generation receives and passes along the legacy of those who have gone before and is made to feel more complete by virtue of the connective tissue of ritual.

For the family group in the painting, the trip to the reservoir of water is probably very much a routine occurrence. But it also has spiritual, social, and other implications that make of the simple ritual something highly desirable. Thus, we see a child who seems happy to accompany mother, and a grandmother who would rather come along than stay at home. Even monotonous chores with their menial and repetitive nature can heal and comfort when loved ones are at our side.

In The Church of Jesus Christ of Latter-day Saints there is not a great deal of public ritual. The administration of the sacrament and the ordinance of baptism are about the only public experiences that have been ritualized through set prayers and formal actions. In the temples of the Church, however, all of the ordinances are highly ritualistic. The repetition of these sacred ordinances becomes a meditative mantra for those who experience them often, and there is great healing in this routine.

If a family had no shared rituals to call its own but those of the sacrament, baptism, and the ordinances of the temple, the family would still be grounded in a very meaningful tradition. If, however, there are added the enriching routines of daily life, family bonds become all the stronger. Family prayer, family scripture study, family playtimes and mealtimes woven into the fabric of our formal spiritual life make for a wonderful composition of family binding— cloth that will bring comfort, warmth, and a sense of belonging to each member.

Some wonder why the Church emphasizes so much the

traditional family of father, mother, and children. Surely it is because this form of family represents the ideal. A happy home life with all roles filled and functioning comes nearer to heaven than any other kind of human existence. The traditional family setting offers the greatest hope for the realization of all the blessings associated with family life. The more complete the family, the more potential there is for individual and group healing and happiness.

POLLUTED OR LIVING WATER?

The mother figure in the painting is carrying a jug, as if she would fill it with the murky water of the pool and take it home to meet the needs of those who live under her roof. We might assume they would use it for cooking, for washing, and for drinking, with little apparent regard for the cleanliness of the water.

The earliest inhabitants of Jerusalem would likely have obtained their water from wells of pure water and clean-running streams. As the city grew and matured, the sources of water became incorporated into the maze of narrow, winding streets and close-set dwellings. Human and animal pollutions made their way into the water supply, but the people continued to use it.

How ironic that the source of pure and living water is standing within a few steps of the family in the painting. From Bloch's depiction, we have no reason to believe that any of these three recognized Jesus as the well from which, if they drank with sincerity, they would never thirst again.

As children, parents, and grandparents of today, it would be well for us to consider the sources from which we draw our nourishment. Not just food and water, of course, but that which nourishes our minds and spirits, as well. Do we occasionally fill ourselves with fare from polluted pools?

In modern times, we are faced with the many pollutions of a supposedly mature society. They are all around us in over-abundance. Our very homes are wired with readily available means of bringing in information and images both good and bad. Like the people of Jerusalem who came to the pool of Bethesda because it was close by their lodgings and offered an easy place from which to fill their jugs, we have become accustomed to getting our spiritual and physical nourishment from sources close at hand and so common we hardly give them a second thought. Familiarity and ready access can result in a foolish acceptance of dangerous rations. Like dirty water, these may give us a temporary feeling of satisfaction, but they also surely poison our souls.

In my name they shall

heal the sick.

—DOCTRINE AND COVENANTS 84:68

The story is told of a village in Africa where, following their daily work and evening meal, the people would gather around an open fire and listen to the stories of the elders. There was a wonderful closeness among village members. The adults loved sharing the tales of their earlier years and of their revered ancestors. The children learned the stories and internalized the lessons derived from them. These lessons taught the foundational values for the village—honesty, hard work, and loyalty. A sense of belonging and shared legacy was enjoyed by all.

As their society matured, modern technology came to the village. Eventually the gatherings around the fireside dwindled as individual families remained in their huts to watch satellite TV. The stories of honored ancestors were replaced by sitcoms and movies of little lasting worth. Some of the shows were filthy. The values of the village began to shift from those that had guided them for generations to a form of media mindlessness, which had no basis in the longstanding and meaningful traditions of the village. The people lost much of their attachment to what really mattered in life.

Such is the lot of those who drink from polluted pools. They will thirst again sooner than they think and will have to return frequently for another dissatisfying draught of artificial nourishment. But those who return to the real thing, the true source of life and the fountain of clean, living water will be blessed. For as He promised the woman coming for water at another well, "Whosoever drinketh of this water shall thirst again: But whosoever drinketh of the water that I shall give him shall never thirst; but the water that I shall give him shall be in him a well of water springing up into everlasting life" (John 4:13–14).

The healing influence of the Lord comes to those who free

themselves from the pollutions of the world and make their dwelling with Him. We sometimes refer to this as being "in the world, but not of the world." We cannot escape the essential demands of life nor the strife, turmoil, sickness, and vulnerability of mortality, but we can lessen their effects by seeking after the Lord and nourishing ourselves at His table. "For the Lamb which is in the midst of the throne shall feed [us], and shall lead [us] unto living fountains of waters: and God shall wipe away all tears from [our] eyes" (Revelation 7:17).

Mother's Vital Role in Healing

Although the mother in the painting appears oblivious to the presence of the Savior, the position in which Bloch places her suggests that he recognizes the essential role of mothers in strengthening their families. Notice in the painting that a line drawn downward from the mother's hand holding the jug, on the angle of her upraised arm, leads directly to the lame man. A similar line drawn on the angle of the Savior's outstretched right arm will meet the line from the mother right at the lame man. Perhaps the message of the artist is that righteous mothers are as saviors to their families. They bring a power of love and healing that is second only to that of the Master Himself. From the nourishing hand of a loving mother, joined with the beckoning hand of the Lord, comes a healing element that can soften the difficult experiences of life and lead us to peace in this life and eternal joy in the life to come. Righteous mothers work in partnership with the Savior in the process of giving mortal life. Their influence never ceases to bear the fruit of love, faith, and hope, all of which bring healing to the heart.

Mothers often have a special sense of what is required to meet the needs of individual members of the family. Children seem to be particularly aware of this. Little ones generally look to mother for the healing attention that seems so important when there is a cut finger or a broken heart.

The child in the painting appears to derive from the touch of Mother's hem a blessing similar to that which came to the New Testament woman with the issue of blood, who sought to touch the hem of the Master Healer and be healed from her malady. The woman said to herself, "If I may but touch his garment, I shall be whole" (Matthew 9:21). So children, when they are in need, often want to touch or get in touch with their mother, that they may receive of her wisdom, understanding, and patient kindness and be whole.

President Gordon B. Hinckley said, "As I look back upon my life and think of the wonder of the companion who walked so long

Even the severe tests of health or a handicapped or disabled body can refine a soul for the glorious day of restoration and healing which surely will come.

—BOYD K. PACKER

beside me, I cannot get over the tremendous influence that she had on me. She was the mother of my children. She gave them life. She nurtured them. She guided them through their formative years. She loved them and dreamed of them and prayed for them. She was so wise and good. She just seemed to have present in her all of the good qualities of her most sterling forebears."[27]

President Hinckley also shared this humorous story of his beloved wife: "My children are now all grown. . . . But when they call and I answer the phone, they say, 'How are you?' And before I can answer, they ask, 'Is Mother there?'"[28]

There Is Healing in Closeness

Separation anxiety is a real issue for many young children. They can become very upset when circumstances require that they be separated from their mother or other significant caregiver. For infants, this may be manifest in crying when mother is out of sight. For older children, the experience of going to school without mother can be very traumatic. Many of us remember the anxiety we felt when we couldn't immediately see mother or father and felt "lost" in the grocery store or some other public place. Thus we see the tendency for many children to cling to a parent when they feel insecure.

As children grow older, their need for closeness and security does not go away. It just takes on different forms. They may not want constant companionship, but they do need praise, validation, and love from their parents. Even when a desire for independence is expressed, a young person will still be grateful for a sense of warmth and acceptance at home.

In the marriage relationship, closeness is also essential. Successful marriage partners enjoy a satisfying level of emotional intimacy. They develop a "marital heart"—they like being together, they trust each other to be kind and understanding, and they are fiercely loyal to one another. Those in troubled marriages sense a distance between one another that is dissatisfying and difficult to overcome. They may not be comfortable in sharing their feelings and may not feel that their spouse really understands and appreciates them.

In loving relationships there is an almost miraculous healing quality that soothes the troubled heart and heals the soul. When we feel loved, much of the fear associated with our daily experience can be overcome. Anxieties and insecurities can be healed if we have faith and trust in the love of those who are close to us. This is particularly true if we include the Lord in our circle of intimate friends. The love of the Savior can heal the wounds that come when other loving relationships are strained.

We may not realize it, but much of the stress and anxiety we face in life can be attributed to separation from the Master Healer and the influence of His Spirit. We may not correlate our lack of personal peace to the distance between ourselves and the Lord, but the greater that distance the less comfort and serenity and healing we will enjoy. The closer we are to the Spirit of the Lord, and thereby the closer we are to Him, the greater will be our peace and happiness.

Separation-induced spiritual anxiety is healed by the administration of the Holy Ghost. We receive of this wonderful Holy Spirit through repentance, obedience, and the prayer of faith. The Great Healer will bind up our wounds, both physical and spiritual, and help us to go forward in His love. By clinging to Him we can feel secure in a sometimes frightening world.

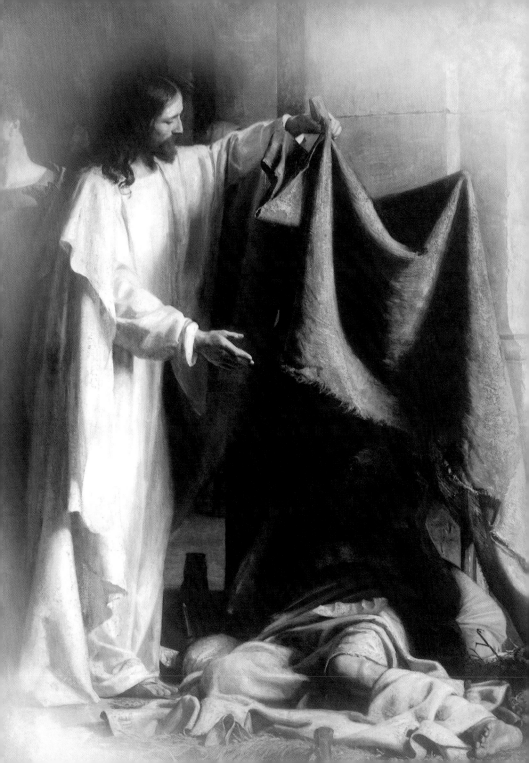

CHAPTER FIVE

Christ and the Healing Moment

The focal point of Carl Bloch's narrative painting is Christ's miraculous healing of the man "which had an infirmity thirty and eight years." Dressed in white and bathed in light, Christ approaches the man who lies huddled in dark shadows beneath a heavy canopy. Jesus lifts the covering, and with that lifting, literally and symbolically heals. The canopy appears to be a visual representation of the maladies that afflict mankind. A step back reveals that the heavy covering appears to be in the form of a cloaked figure with dark hood and hands becoming limp in the Savior's grasp. By showing Christ removing a human-shaped canopy, Bloch visually amplifies the healing process. The dark canopy dissolves into the Savior's reach, and the bright light gradually ascends the man's form. We view the healing *in process* as we literally see dark becoming light, infirm becoming strong, or perhaps sinfulness giving way to repentance. The words of Paul to the Corinthians could describe the dynamics of the scene: "Therefore if any man be in Christ, he is a new creature: old things are passed away; behold, all things are become new" (2 Corinthians 5:17).

Bloch clearly emphasizes Christ as the source of healing. Christ's figure is central, bright, active, and powerful; whereas Bethesda's pool is dark, stagnant, and marginalized. In fact, the water is still enough to capture reflections. Clearly, the pool is not the healer, but merely a reflection of God's healing power. The stone pillars and floors further emphasize the living Christ. Though sturdy, they are man-made, worn and weathered; whereas the Son of God is divine: filled with everlasting grace, power, love, and life. Christ comes to the scene with "healing in his wings" (2 Nephi 25:13). And with His vibrant appearance, all else dissolves into the background.

For the man with an infirmity, the makeshift canopy seems to have been his cover for a long time. Though it provides some shelter and comfort, it also appears to be a hide-out of sorts. It shields the man from light—and perhaps from further heartache and disappointment. Who of us hasn't hidden beneath such a cover at some point in our lives, wanting to be healed but also not wanting to expose ourselves to further injury? Notice the weight of the canopy. It appears heavy. The man does not seem to be able to lift it by himself. He can reach under it, push it to the side, but someone stronger than himself must lift it all the way off. He's too weak to do it on his own. Notice also how the canopy diffuses light. After so many years, the man must be accustomed to dimness. Maybe the reactions of others have driven him farther into the gloomy covering. Sadly, it seems to have become easier to hide in shadows than face the full reality of his condition. Although we don't know the precise nature of his infirmity, we know that it is serious and chronic. For thirty-eight years he has been afflicted. The loosely wrapped rags and bare chest remind us of his vulnerability. A stake, of sorts, is in front of his bed of straw, perhaps once securing the edge of his canopy. The stake is symbolic of his immovable condition, while the food in the basket next to him reminds us of his insatiable hunger for healing.

The man came as close to the water, a symbol of healing, as he could on his own. But like most of us, he needed help to go further. He had faith enough to wait at water's edge for who-knows-how-many of those thirty-eight years. But he was ill-informed and lacking in

While I was lying in my hospital bed . . . I discovered that if I dwelt only upon my pain, it inhibited the healing process. I found that pondering was a very important element in the healing process for both soul and body. Pain brings you to a humility that allows you to ponder. It is an experience I am grateful to have endured.

—ELDER ROBERT D. HALES

support. One wonders how many times he asked for assistance into the pool. Or how many times he was *almost* the first one into the water? Did he ever witness another's healing? Why would he wait so unfailingly by the mystical waters?

As the Savior lifts the canopy, the man seems surprised but also awe-inspired and relieved. The man drops a half-eaten slice of melon as the light of the Lord washes over him. He seems to intuitively recognize the Great Healer for whom he has waited so long. This is his moment of healing! He would not have had the same exultant expression if it were a friend or another stranger who lifted his shroud. Perhaps he has heard the stories around Palestine of a healer come from God who has healed so many others. It may be that he has patiently prayed for the Master Healer to come to him.

Either way, this is the moment for which he has waited. His eyes reveal his heart. They are the pleading, weary eyes of a sincere believer. His eyes are not those of a hardened enemy or a sinful sloth. In the darkness of Bloch's masterful depiction we see his eyes: filled with earnest importuning, heartfelt gratitude, and genuine, awe-inspired faith. The eyes seem to say, "At long last my prayers have been answered; my Savior has come to heal me."

Remarkably, the Savior comes to this man and He comes to this man

Wait for Me; wait—and I will come to heal you.

—Thomas à Kempis

68

first. Jesus has come to perform a miracle and to teach. Clearly, Jesus could discern that the man's heart was believing and humble—or healable. Jesus must have been aware that the man had done all that he could on his own and was in a position to receive the gift of healing. "Seemingly Jesus deliberately sought out a man worthy to be healed so that he might exercise his curative powers on the Sabbath day. The interest and animosity resulting from this Sabbath miracle were such that our Lord gained an attentive, though largely disbelieving congregation of hearers, for what is perhaps his greatest recorded sermon of the relationship of the Father and the Son [see John 5:17–24]," wrote Elder Bruce R. McConkie.[29] That the healing takes place on the Sabbath day is not visually apparent. Those well-versed in scripture would recall this important detail, and perhaps they would most benefit from remembering that the "Son of man is Lord even of the Sabbath day" (Matthew 12:8). While this healing moment opened some hearts to the Savior's saving truths, other self-righteous onlookers became bitter opponents of Jesus and his "Sabbath-breaking."

We join the man being healed in looking earnestly to Jesus, dressed in resplendent white. Our eyes go instantly to the Lord's hands. His left hand gently lifts the canvas; His right hand is upturned and extended in love and compassion. Not the hand of condemnation or reprimand, the gracious hand of Christ is one that has power to heal and save. The open hand manifests His words, "Rise, take up thy bed, and walk." That same loving hand

> *Realize your full dependence upon the Lord and your need to align your life with His teachings. There is really no other way to get lasting healing and peace.*
>
> —ELDER RICHARD G. SCOTT

reaches out to us. That same compassionate voice reassuringly invites us, "Come unto me, all ye that labour and are heavy laden, and I will give you rest. Take my yoke upon you, and learn of me; for I am meek and lowly in heart: and ye shall find rest unto your souls. For my yoke is easy, and my burden is light" (Matthew 11:28–30).

Over and over again we read that the Lord's "hand is stretched out still" (see Isaiah 5:25; 9:12, 17): "And how merciful is our God unto us, for he remembereth the house of Israel, both roots and branches; and he stretches forth his hands unto them all the day long; and they are a stiffnecked and a gainsaying people; but as many as will not harden their hearts shall be saved in the kingdom of God" (Jacob 6:4).

HELP AND HEALING

The Lord wants to help and heal us. His greatest desire is to bless us with strength and joy for the journey of life, with happiness in our hearts and homes, with that comforting peace "which passeth all understanding" (Philippians 4:7).

The Lord also knows that our sojourn through mortality will not be easy—that we will suffer infirmities of body and spirit for which we need healing. He knows with perfect understanding and empathy that life will be filled with some measure of sorrow and heartache, with trials and difficulties (see Mosiah 3:7; Alma 7:12). But He also knows what we need in order to develop the attributes of godliness. As the apostle Paul said, "For our light affliction, which is but for a moment, worketh for us a far more exceeding and eternal weight of glory" (2 Corinthians 4:17). In the eternal scheme of things, even thirty-eight years is but a moment. Clearly, the Lord's way is not always our way or on our timetable (see Isaiah 55:8–9). But His promises are sure.

If we come unto Him, the Lord will not leave us comfortless. Our physical pains and disabilities may not be alleviated, but our spirits can be healed of anger, disappointment, and bitterness. Sometimes, when we feel alone in our suffering, we can find comfort in remembering that loved ones on the other side of the veil watch over us. Elder Jeffrey R. Holland reminded us of the unseen help we have in the face of discouragement: "In the gospel of Jesus Christ you have help from both sides of the veil, and you must never forget that. When disappointment and discouragement strike—and they will—you remember and never forget that if our eyes could be opened we would see horses and chariots of fire as far as the eye can see riding at reckless speed to come to our protection. They will always be there, these armies of heaven, in defense of Abraham's seed."[30]

Indeed, Jesus' outstretched hand reaches to us in love and compassion, ready to lift and succor and heal. By His own voice, the Lord declared to the faithful, "I will also ease the burdens which are put upon your shoulders, that even you cannot feel them upon your backs, even while you are in bondage; . . . that ye may stand as witnesses for me hereafter, and that ye may know of a surety that I, the Lord God, do visit my people in their afflictions." And in fulfillment of that wonderful promise, "the Lord did strengthen them that they could bear up their burdens with ease, and they did submit cheerfully and with patience to all the will of the Lord" (Mosiah 24:14–15).

The Lord's gospel plan for us is to continue to become more like Him, and ultimately to live the quality of life that He Himself enjoys, even eternal life—His greatest gift (see D&C 14:7). But, first, we must seek Him and His healing power.

THE LORD IS THE GREAT HEALER

Jesus Christ came into the world as the Master Healer of our souls. Turning the pages of scripture reveals how regularly and often he not only healed people of their physical infirmities but also cast out the evil spirits that afflicted them. Some might think there were an awful lot of people possessed of evil spirits during Jesus' mortal ministry. And there were. But there are no fewer now, and in all likelihood, more. In today's world, we may have more labels for the evil influences that canker souls. Now, we say someone is "angry," "bitter," "mean-spirited," "unforgiving," "selfish," "materialistic," or worse. Conversely, we all know someone who was once entrapped by such an evil attitude who is now free from that spiritual bondage. The evil influence has literally been cast out of them as they have repented, lived more fully the gospel of Jesus Christ, and actively pursued the path of faith and righteousness. In every sense, they have been healed.

In the Book of Mormon, just prior to the resurrected Lord's coming to the Americas, the prophet Nephi went about preaching the gospel of Jesus Christ and witnessing the healing of many souls: "And as many as had devils cast out from them, and were healed of their sicknesses and their infirmities,

Many of you suffer needlessly from carrying heavy burdens because you do not open your hearts to the healing power of the Lord.

—RICHARD G. SCOTT

did truly manifest unto the people that they had been wrought upon by the Spirit of God, and had been healed; and they did show forth signs also and did do some miracles among the people" (3 Nephi 7:22). The Lord, through his authorized servants, accomplishes such healings today.

Each time we make a decision to obey the Lord by obeying His latter-day prophets, we move along the path to healing—and happiness. We will always be blessed as we heed the counsel of apostles and prophets (see D&C 130:20–21). The prophet Jacob teaches: "the pleasing word of God . . . healeth the wounded soul" (Jacob 2:8). As we put exclamation points instead of question marks after the admonitions of our leaders, as we hear and hearken to their counsel, sweet peace will distill upon our souls. We will come to know that the pathway to safety, serenity, and happiness comes from submitting our will to the will of the Lord.

I am the Lord that

healeth thee.

—EXODUS 15:26

When we choose to follow the Lord by trusting in the counsel of His appointed representatives, the Lord is bound to bless us (see D&C 21:4–6). President James E. Faust taught, "In my lifetime, there have been very few occasions when I questioned the wisdom and inspiration given by key priesthood leaders. I have always tried to follow their counsel, whether I agreed with it or not. I have come to know that most of the time they were in tune with the Spirit and I was not. The safe course is to sustain our priesthood leaders and let God judge their actions. . . .

"I do not speak of blind obedience, but rather the obedience of faith, which supports and sustains decisions with confidence that they are inspired. I advocate being more in tune with the Spirit so we may feel a confirming witness of the truthfulness of the direction we receive from our priesthood leaders. There is great safety and peace in supporting our priesthood leaders in their decisions."[31]

We as Saints have never believed in blind obedience, because in all the commands of God we have the ability to choose, we have complete soul freedom and moral agency (see Helaman 14:30–31). God will force no person to heaven, and the devil cannot compel us to hell. We are always and forever free to choose. But when we choose the path the Savior trod, we find hope and healing. When we choose to follow the Lord's anointed servants, we find peace. Like the man under the canopy in Bloch's painting, we, too, are lifted out of darkness as we learn and then live the gospel of Jesus Christ.

FAITH TO BE HEALED

Oftentimes, prior to a miraculous healing, the Savior asked, "Believe ye that I am able to do this?" (Matthew 9:28). The implications are: (1) the Lord could not force a healing; the person had to *want* to be healed; and (2) the person had to believe in Jesus and His power to heal. Each of these components is vital to healing: wanting to be healed and having the faith to turn to the Lord for that healing. For example, the prophet Alma asked the remorseful Zeezrom: "Believest thou in the power of Christ unto salvation?" And when Zeezrom responded in the affirmative, Alma further taught: "If thou believest in the redemption of Christ thou canst be healed" (Alma 15: 6, 8).

> *I am the way, the truth, and the life: no man cometh unto the Father, but by me.*
>
> —JOHN 14:6

The world offers all sorts of comforts and allurements that may bring temporary relief from spiritual pain, but only Christ—His teachings, gospel, and priesthood power—can truly heal. Only He can bring lasting peace and spiritual well-being. Feelings of real hope and abiding joy cannot come any other way. But we must be willing to take the Master Healer's prescriptions for pain, which is this: "Enter ye in at the strait gate: for wide is the gate, and broad is the way, that leadeth to destruction, and many there be which go in thereat: Because strait is the gate, and narrow is the way, which leadeth unto life, and few there be that find it" (Matthew 7:13–14).

Why do "few" find the path to healing? It could be because the pathway is paved with faith—vibrant, active, life-changing faith. Possessing such faith is prerequisite to spiritual healing. Elder James E. Talmage taught: "Faith is of itself a principle of power; and by its presence or absence, by its fulness or paucity, even the Lord was and is influenced, and in great measure controlled, in the bestowal or withholding of blessings; for He ministers according to law, and not with caprice or uncertainty. . . .

"Passive belief on the part of a would-be recipient of blessing is insufficient; only when it is vitalized into active faith is it a power; so also of one who ministers in the authority given of God, mental and spiritual energy must be operative if the service is to be effective."[32]

Oftentimes, people wonder why the Lord can't bestow upon them the blessing or the answer they seek when they are not willing to do their part by keeping His commandments. It takes time and maturity to understand the connection between obedience to God's law and faith in His purposes. In other words, faith precedes the miracle. Obedience invites healing because obedience breeds faith.

Indeed, the most lasting and effectual healings come from seeking and submitting to God's will in our lives and remaining steadfast in faith until the end. The words to the beloved hymn, "How Gentle God's Commands," remind us of God's love and His willingness to heal our hearts. We set the process in motion by exercising faith.

> *How gentle God's commands!*
> *How kind his precepts are!*
> *Come, cast your burdens on the Lord*
> *And trust his constant care.*

Beneath his watchful eye,
His Saints securely dwell;
That hand which bears all nature up
Shall guard his children well.

Why should this anxious load
Press down your weary mind?
Haste to your Heav'nly Father's throne
And sweet refreshment find.

His goodness stands approved,
Unchanged from day to day;
I'll drop my burden at his feet
And bear a song away.[33]

The key to the kind of healing that allows us to "bear a song away" is faith. The steady and stable string of faith empowers the kite of healing to take flight.

Another implication of the question, "Believe ye that I am able to do this?" is meekness. By turning our well-being over to the Lord's protective care, we put ourselves in a position to be healed. Such meekness is not developed haphazardly. We become "heal-able" as we become "submissive, meek, humble, patient, full of love, willing to submit to all things which the Lord seeth fit to inflict upon [us], even as a child doth submit to his father" (Mosiah 3:19). Meekness is strength; it is confidence in the Lord and His purposes. "The questions Why me? Why our family? Why now?

are usually unanswerable questions," said Elder Robert D. Hales. "These questions detract from our spirituality and can destroy our faith. We need to spend our time and energy building our faith by turning to the Lord and asking for strength to overcome the pains and trials of this world and to endure to the end for greater understanding. . . .

"Our Savior knows the heart of each of us. He knows the pains of our hearts. If we seek the truth, develop faith in Him, and, if necessary, sincerely repent, we will receive a spiritual change of heart which only comes from our Savior. Our hearts will become new again."[34] Truly, we can be given a new and meek heart as we earnestly turn to the Lord (see Ezekiel 11:1–20). And miraculously, even if the source of pain does not change or go away, our hearts can heal and we can feel the Lord's love.

I will take the stony heart out of their flesh, and will give them an heart of flesh.

—EZEKIEL 11:19

One woman endured months of rehabilitation after back surgery only to find herself more and more crippled by pain. She spent days on end flat in bed, completely dependent upon the kindness of others. She was given priesthood blessings. She fasted and prayed but found no relief from the physical pain. Eventually, a second and more complicated operation in another state revealed the cause of her discomfort. But long before finding relief from physical pain, she experienced a complete spiritual recovery. She spoke of how her heart turned to her Relief Society sisters, how her love increased for her family, how her heart turned to the Lord. She stopped feeling sorry for herself and found ways in her weakened condition to express gratitude and reach out to others. She was healed both physically and spiritually, but her spiritual healing was so complete that her physical recovery became less and less important. Oftentimes the spiritual healing precedes or accompanies the physical healing—as our hearts are softened through submission to the Lord, healing becomes possible. Indeed, the spiritual healing—a softened and submissive heart—may be the most important healing of all.

A wise physician told his patient, "There is no cure for what you have, but there *is* healing." The physician understood that sometimes the healing we need does not come from medical treatment. Healing of the soul comes from unselfish concern for others, from integrity and goodness, from repentance and forgiveness. Every time we reach past personal concerns to encourage and lift others, we can experience a healing of the heart. When we feel anguish or animosity, we can find healing by letting go of anger and blame. When we feel troubled and afraid, we can find peace in sincere prayer and in the words of scriptures and hymns. When we feel as though we can't face another day, we can find courage in sweet assurances and the quiet confidence of family and friends.

Humility, empathy, and kindness are healing ointments. Heartfelt meditation can soothe the worried soul. Even the beauties of nature can lift our spirits and help us look to a higher source for healing. The Lord's promise is sure: "I have heard thy prayer, I have seen thy tears: behold, I will heal thee" (2 Kings 20:5).

May His healing

power sustain you.

—PRESIDENT GORDON B. HINCKLEY

Healing can come as we patiently wait for the Lord. But more often than not, we must proactively search for Him. We must be determined in our desire to find Him. He knocks at the door, but the doorknob is always on our side of the door.

HEALING HAPPENS AT THE WATER'S EDGE

It seems no accident that Bloch painted the man who was healed as waiting at the water's edge. As if to signify that the man had gone as far as he could on his own and was now dependent on the Lord's saving grace, the painting shows how we must endure in faith in order to be healed.

Sometimes we can be so discouraged by pains and problems that Satan would like us to think that we can't even get to the water's edge, that it is not worth the effort. One way we get strength to go to the water's edge, or to endure in faith, is by remembering our inherent worth as children of God. "Each of us should remember that he or she is a son or daughter of God, endowed with faith, gifted with courage, and guided by prayer. Our eternal destiny is before us," said President Thomas S. Monson. "At times many of us let that enemy of achievement—even the culprit 'self-defeat'—dwarf our aspirations, smother our dreams, cloud our vision, and impair our lives. The enemy's voice whispers in our ears, 'You can't do it.' 'You're too young.' 'You're too old.' 'You're nobody.' This is when we remember that we are created in the image of God. Reflection on this truth provides a profound sense of strength and power."[35]

We go to the water's edge as we strive to keep the commandments and kindly encourage others to do the same (see 1 Nephi 17:15). As we trust the Lord, as we serve and bless others, as we forget ourselves and go to work, we put ourselves in a position to be healed. If you and I are to be healed, we must acquaint ourselves with the life and teachings of the Master Healer. We find Him and his healing power each time we reach out to others in love. We find Him as we earnestly turn to the scriptures, as we humbly fast and pray, as we sincerely ponder the life of the Master Healer and the things of eternity. Whenever we come unto the Light of the World with repentant hearts, we are taken out of darkness and see things as with new eyes (see John 9:25). Like the resplendent white of Jesus' robe in Bloch's depiction, God's commandments—when heeded—can light our souls.

Perhaps nothing brings us to the water's edge and invites

healing more than heartfelt repentance. When we make a course correction, not only do we get back on the path, but we gain a more firm testimony of the rightness of that path. By humbly admitting the error of our ways, we both renew our *resolve* to stay on the path and our *ability* to do so. We gain ultimate victory by surrendering our willful and wanton nature to the Lord. The Lord himself pointed to the connection between repentance and healing. He pled with the Nephites, and each of us: "Will ye not now return unto me, and repent of your sins, and be converted, that I may heal you?" (3 Nephi 9:13).

Such sincere repentance is best demonstrated in long-term commitments to follow the Lord and trust in His ways. If we go to the water's edge filled with soulful repentance, we will drink the clear waters of forgiveness. But we must be willing to do whatever the Lord requires. The great missionary Ammon taught: "But if ye will turn to the Lord with full purpose of heart, and put your trust in him, and serve him with all diligence of mind, if ye do this, he will, according to his own will and pleasure, deliver you out of bondage" (Mosiah 7:33). We may be suffering the bondage of pain and heartache, the burden of sin and temptation, the oppression of strained relationships, grudges, and regret. We are released from such bondage—even healed—by turning to the Lord, by believing and trusting Him, by obeying Him with all our heart.

The key to an enduring healing is an enduring trust in the Lord. Nephi of old exemplified such trust. He said of their journey

As a family . . . we don't worry as we would if we hadn't felt the transcendent reach and healing power of Jesus Christ.

—SHERI L. DEW

to the Promised Land: "And if it so be that the children of men keep the commandments of God he doth nourish them, and strengthen them, and provide means whereby they can accomplish the thing which he has commanded them; wherefore, he did provide means for us while we did sojourn in the wilderness" (1 Nephi 17:3). Our "sojourn in the wilderness" may take a much different form than Nephi's, but the means the Lord provides for our spiritual survival would be much the same as Nephi's: trusting in the word of God, sincere prayer, prophetic leadership, and refining experiences.

Even with strong faith and trust, even when we have set up camp on the water's edge, our life will not be free from pain or difficulty. Mortality, with all its joys and adventures, is by definition full of heartache and sorrow. When pain, anguish, and trials come, stay close to the Savior. "Wait upon the Lord, . . . look for him" (Isaiah 8:17; 2 Nephi 18:17). "They that wait upon the Lord shall renew their strength; they shall mount up with wings as eagles; they shall run, and not be weary; and they shall walk, and not faint" (Isaiah 40:31). If we trust the Lord and patiently endure to the end, healing will come in the Lord's time and in the Lord's way.

The Lord's mercy and compassion is extended to *all* who do their part to "come to the water's edge" with faith. Not just the physically challenged but also the mentally and spiritually distressed can be healed as they draw near to the Savior. And when they are healed, they will rejoice and feel grateful, just as the Nephites of old: "And they did all, both they who had been healed and they who were whole, bow down at his feet, and did worship him; and as many as could come for the multitude did kiss his feet, insomuch that they did bathe his feet with their tears" (3 Nephi 17:10).

CHAPTER SIX

The Healer's Art

Savior, may I learn to love thee,

Walk the path that thou hast shown,

Pause to help and lift another,

Finding strength beyond my own.

Savior, may I learn to love thee—

Lord, I would follow thee.

Who am I to judge another

When I walk imperfectly?

In the quiet heart is hidden

Sorrow that the eye can't see.

Who am I to judge another?

Lord, I would follow thee.

I would be my brother's keeper;
I would learn the healer's art.
To the wounded and the weary
I would show a gentle heart.
I would be my brother's keeper—
Lord, I would follow thee.

Savior, may I love my brother
As I know thou lovest me,
Find in thee my strength, my beacon,
For thy servant I would be.
Savior, may I love my brother—
Lord, I would follow thee.[36]

To follow Jesus is to learn the Healer's art. Belief in His divine gift of healing keeps us going during difficult times; it gives hope that can soothe our souls and help us endure trials. To all who suffer pain, distress, and disappointment, to all weighed down by sin, sorrow, and resentment, the Savior simply says, "Come unto me."

What does it mean to come unto Jesus?

We come unto Him when, in meekness, in diligent obedience, in an attitude of sincere seeking, we lay our will and willfulness on the altar of submission and wait upon the Lord. Healing will come in the Lord's way and on His timetable, but it will come. If we

replace the word *peace* with *healing* in a familiar passage of scripture, we see how the Lord stands ready to help: "[Healing] I leave
with you, my [healing] I give unto you: not as the world giveth,
give I unto you. Let not your heart be troubled, neither let it be
afraid" (John 14:27).

But just as surely as Christ desires to heal us, the adversary of
righteousness opposes our healing. The great deceiver whispers in
our ear, "Healing is not possible; you have made too many mistakes," "It's too hard," or "Healing is not available to one such as
you." He would have us give in to discouragement and hopelessness, give in to sinfulness and apathy, give in to the forces of inertia
that lead us downward into despair. The father of lies wants us to
become embittered by our heartaches and resentful toward any who
appear to have experienced the healing balm. More than anything,
the enemy of righteousness wants us to believe that Christ is power-
less to save, unable to help and heal. But the devil has been "a liar
from the beginning" (D&C 93:25); in him is no hope, no help, no
healing.

When he whispers his falsehoods, we must remember the
inspiring words of Helaman: "And now, my sons, remember,
remember that it is upon the rock of our Redeemer, who is Christ,
the Son of God, that ye must build your foundation; that when the
devil shall send forth his mighty winds, yea, his shafts in the whirl-
wind, yea, when all his hail and his mighty storm shall beat upon
you, it shall have no power over you to drag you down to the gulf

of misery and endless woe, because of the rock upon which ye are built, which is a sure foundation, a foundation whereon if men build they cannot fall" (Helaman 5:12). Christ is the sure foundation upon which we can rest our hope.

His promises are sure. After inviting the Nephites to come unto Him and be healed, He assured them, "Behold, mine arm of mercy is extended towards you, and whosoever will come, him will I receive; and blessed are those who come unto me" (3 Nephi 9:13–14). In our dispensation, He likewise promised, "Be patient in tribulation until I come; and, behold, I come quickly, and my reward is with me, and they who have sought me early shall find rest to their souls" (D&C 54:10).

It takes courage to believe in the divine gift of healing when our soul may be crippled with pain. It takes faith not to be distracted by the temporal trappings or quick fixes the world offers. It takes strength to endure the suffering that precedes and often accompanies healing. To be healed requires careful spiritual preparation. Before the light of heaven can infuse our soul with healing and peace, we must open our eyes, soften our heart, and desire to become truly converted (see Matthew 13:15; John 12:40). Trusting in the Lord's healing hand is a lifelong process that requires developing our faith in Him, recognizing the inestimable value of His atoning sacrifice, and striving more fully to live a Christlike life.

WE ALL NEED HEALING

Healing is a process of restoring and becoming whole, repairing, mending, and putting back together. We all need help and healing—every one of us. Some of our wounds are obvious, easily seen. Other wounds are hidden, almost invisible, and frequently ignored. Perhaps we think we can move past the pain simply through sheer willpower or positive thinking. But to be made whole, we must recognize both our need for healing and the source of authentic relief.

> *In Nazareth, the narrow road,*
> *That tires the feet and steals the breath,*
> *Passes the place where once abode*
> *The Carpenter of Nazareth.*
>
> *And up and down the dusty way*
> *The village folk would often wend;*
> *And on the bench, beside Him, lay*
> *Their broken things for Him to mend.*
>
> *The maiden with the doll she broke,*
> *The woman with the broken chair,*
> *The man with broken plough, or yoke,*
> *Said, "Can you mend it, Carpenter?"*
>
> *And each received the thing he sought,*
> *In yoke or plough, or chair, or doll;*

The broken thing which each had brought
Returned again a perfect whole.

So, up the hill the long years through,
With heavy step and wistful eye,
The burdened souls their way pursue,
Uttering each the plaintive cry:

"O Carpenter of Nazareth,
This heart, that's broken past repair,
This life, that's shattered nigh to death,
Oh, can You mend them, Carpenter?"

And by His kind and ready hand,
His own sweet life is woven through
Our broken lives, until they stand
A New Creation—"all things new."

The shattered idols of my heart,
Desire, ambition, hope, and faith,
Mould Thou into the perfect part,
O Carpenter of Nazareth!"[37]

Whether our wounds are gaping or minuscule, whether our heartaches are large or small, we are all broken, all less than perfectly whole, all in need of the Master Healer.

THE LESSONS OF PAIN

"In this mortal life, each of us is going to experience pain in one form or another," said Elder Robert D. Hales. "Pain may come from an accident or from a painful medical condition. We may feel deep pain from the mourning that appropriately comes with the loss of a loved one or the loss of affection from one we hold dear. Pain may come from feeling lonely or depressed. It often comes as a result of our disobedience to the commandments of God, but it also comes to those who are doing all they can to keep their lives in line with the example of the Savior. . . .

"My dear brothers and sisters, when pain, tests, and trials come in life, draw near to the Savior. 'Wait upon the Lord, . . . look for him' (Isaiah 8:17; 2 Nephi 18:17). 'They that wait upon the Lord shall renew their strength; they shall mount up with wings as eagles; they shall run, and not be weary; and they shall walk, and not faint' (Isaiah 40:31). Healing comes in the Lord's time and the Lord's way; be patient.

"Our Savior waits for us to come to Him through our scripture study, pondering, and prayer to our Heavenly Father. Great blessings and lessons come from overcoming adversity. As we are strengthened and healed, we can then lift and strengthen others with our faith. May we be instruments in the Lord's hands in blessing the lives of those in pain.

"I give you my testimony that God lives and that Jesus is the

Christ and that He waits for us to come to Him to give us counsel and compassionate caring."[38]

Healing usually takes time. Hope and energy are drained drop by drop, by life's daily stresses and strains, causing spiritual and emotional fatigue. Similarly, healing is very often a gradual process of growth and recovery. Often not until years later do we see the healing that took place over time and in miraculous ways.

Forty years ago, a young man fell from a tall tree and was left essentially paralyzed on the right side of his body. As an active teenager and catcher on the high school baseball team, his body was young and strong. Instantly, he became broken. Today, he has no use of his right arm. He walks with a bit of a limp. But among so many other things, he plays the piano beautifully with one hand. He and his wife have raised an impressive family of faithful children. They have built the kingdom of God in wonderful ways. He will tell you how he once struggled with questions, "Why me?" and "What will the future bring?"

But now, with the wisdom of maturity and faithfulness, he talks about the blessing the fall was in his life. He has learned about empathy and compassion; he has turned his life over to the Savior and accessed His healing atonement. He now says, "The fall I took as a young man has blessed my life. The lessons I have learned I would not trade for anything. This was part of God's plan for me, and if I could change that day of forty years ago I wouldn't." Although his body is not fully healed, his heart is. His heart is full of love and understanding, caring and compassion. His healing process, borne on the enabling and healing power of the Atonement, has restored his soul and made him whole.

As this good man learned, trials and tragedies are a part of life—an important part. Were it not for the sorrow, we could not comprehend joy; were it not for the pain, we would not appreciate relief and peace. Pain schools us and prepares our souls for eternity. And pain can bring us to the source of all healing, Jesus Christ.

Elder Orson F. Whitney of the Quorum of the Twelve Apostles wrote, "No pain that we suffer . . . is wasted. It ministers to our education, to the development of . . . patience, faith, fortitude and humility. All that we suffer . . . , especially when we endure it patiently, builds up our characters, purifies our hearts, expands our souls, and makes us more tender and charitable, more worthy to be called the children of God . . . and it is through sorrow and suffering, toil and tribulation, that we gain the education that we come here to acquire and which will make us more like our Father and Mother in heaven."[39]

HEALING AND GRATITUDE

We can find peace; we can find rest to our souls in Christ. We can change and be made whole—whatever the problem, whatever the difficulty—because Christ atoned for our sins and shortcomings and sufferings. Isaiah's poignant description of the Savior's healing power touches our hearts even as it inspires:

"He is despised and rejected of men; a man of sorrows, and acquainted with grief: and we hid as it were our faces from him; he was despised, and we esteemed him not.

"Surely he hath borne our griefs, and carried our sorrows: yet we did esteem him stricken, smitten of God, and afflicted.

"But he was wounded for our transgressions, he was bruised for our iniquities: the chastisement of our peace was upon him; and with his stripes we are healed" (Isaiah 53:3–5).

Our hearts are filled with thanksgiving as we contemplate the majesty and power of the Lord's healing hand. Our gratitude knows no bounds as we look patiently to the Lord for help and healing. Truly, to be filled with profound gratefulness for the Lord, his healing balm, and comforting love, is part of the healing process. And when we are healed by His touch, we must respond as did the leper who was cleansed by the Lord:

"And as [Jesus] entered into a certain village, there met him ten men that were lepers, which stood afar off: And they lifted up their voices, and said, Jesus, Master, have mercy on us. And when he saw them, he said unto them, Go shew yourselves unto the priests. And it came to pass, that, as they went, they were cleansed. And one of them, when he saw that he was healed, turned back, and with a loud voice glorified God, And fell down on his face at his feet, giving him thanks: and he was a Samaritan. And Jesus answering said, Were there not ten cleansed? but where are the nine? There are not found that returned to give glory to God, save this stranger. And he said unto him, Arise, go thy way: thy faith hath made thee whole" (Luke 17:12–19). Like the leper who returned to give thanks after partaking of Christ's healing power, our healing becomes "whole" when we are filled with profound gratitude.

Then, after we are healed, our feeling of indebtedness to God impels us to help others find healing. Our hearts are drawn to the welfare of others, and like Jesus, we want to go about "doing good" (Acts 10:38). We want to practice the healer's art and encourage, forgive, and lift others. We want to reach out with tenderness to the lonely, the downtrodden, and the forgotten.

HE KNOWS US

In the most intimate and personal way, the Lord is our shepherd. He knows His sheep; He knows best how to take care of us and protect us, how to nurture and lead us along, how to help and heal us. Speaking metaphorically of us, Jesus said, "I am the good shepherd, and know my sheep. . . . My sheep hear my voice, and I know them, and they follow me" (John 10:14, 27).

To His followers who lived in a land of shepherds, the metaphor was compelling and unforgettable: "The Lord is my shepherd; I shall not want." As lambs, He leads us to green pastures and still waters, to all that is nourishing and nurturing. When we are buffeted by temptation and fear, "he leadeth [us] in the paths of righteousness." When we are broken and in need of mending, "he restoreth [the] soul." Though walking through deep darkness in the valley of sorrow, "[we] will fear no evil." Though we are stretched by the tests and trials of life, our cup can run over with thanksgiving for His watchful care and tender mercies. Only because of the Good Shepherd, "goodness and mercy shall follow [us] all the days of [our] life."[40] When we are healed, our deepest desire and most earnest yearning is to "dwell in the house of the Lord forever" (Psalm 23).

May the healing hand of the Lord attend us this day and always. May we each find comfort and blessing, peace and joy, faith and hope in Jesus Christ. And may we be inspired to help others find this same sweet assurance in the Healer's art.

Some Ways to Facilitate Personal Healing

Obtain a blessing from a worthy priesthood holder.

———•———

Attend the temple. Ponder the everlasting things; "Treasure these things up
in your [heart] and let the solemnities of eternity rest upon your [mind]"
(D&C 43:34); listen to the promptings of the Holy Spirit.

———•———

Pray.

———•———

Read and ponder the scriptures. Highlight verses that
relate to your circumstances.

———•———

Read any uplifting and motivating book.
Underline meaningful passages.

———•———

Spend time outdoors enjoying the beauties of nature.
Go for a walk, take a drive, go to a park and watch children play,
or simply listen to the call of a bird, the whisper of the wind, or
the splashing of a stream.

———•———

Record your experiences and feelings in a journal,
either handwritten or on a computer.

———•———

Paint or draw something in a sketchbook.

———•———

Take stock of your life and contemplate what is most important to you.
Count your blessings.

———•———

Watch a movie that calms your soul, makes you laugh, or
recounts some inspiring event.

———•———

Compose an essay or a poem.

———•———

Listen to music that soothes your heart and lifts your mood,
or read the words of a favorite hymn.

———•———

Write a letter to yourself in which you pour out your feelings.

———◆———

*Talk to an empathetic family member or friend who
will sometimes just listen, other times give wise counsel and
encouragement—someone who can make you laugh
and give you proper perspective.*

———◆———

*Visit with your bishop, who is entitled to revelation in your behalf. Seek his
help to resolve past mistakes or overcome current difficulties.*

———◆———

*Perform meaningful service. Put off thinking of yourself
and find ways to help others.*

———◆———

*Get help from a professional. Properly prescribed medication
may help relieve anxiety, depression, or pain and restore balance.*

———◆———

*With guidance from your physician, take responsibility for
your own healing. Consider the benefits of exercise and nutrition.*

Scriptural Answers to Some Questions about Healing

BY WHAT POWER ARE WE HEALED?

"And he spake unto me again, saying: Look! And I looked, and I beheld the Lamb of God going forth among the children of men. And I beheld multitudes of people who were sick, and who were afflicted with all manner of diseases, and with devils and unclean spirits; and the angel spake and showed all these things unto me. And they were healed by the power of the Lamb of God; and the devils and the unclean spirits were cast out."

(1 Nephi 11:31)

"And, behold, a woman, which was diseased with an issue of blood twelve years, came behind *him,* and touched the hem of his garment:

"For she said within herself, If I may but touch his garment, I shall be whole.

"But Jesus turned him about, and when he saw her, he said, Daughter, be of good comfort; thy faith hath made thee whole. And the woman was made whole from that hour."

(Matthew 9:20–22)

DO HEALING MIRACLES OCCUR IN MODERN TIMES?

"And again I speak unto you who deny the revelations of God, and say that they are done away, that there are no revelations, nor prophecies, nor gifts, nor healing, nor speaking with tongues, and the interpretation of tongues;

"Behold I say unto you, he that denieth these things knoweth not the gospel of Christ; yea, he has not read the scriptures; if so, he does not understand them.

"For do we not read that God is the same yesterday, today, and forever, and in him there is no variableness neither shadow of changing?

"And now, if ye have imagined up unto yourselves a god who doth vary, and in whom there is shadow of changing, then have ye imagined up unto yourselves a god who is not a God of miracles.

"But behold, I will show unto you a God of miracles, even the God of Abraham, and the God of Isaac, and the God of Jacob; and it is that same God who created the heavens and the earth, and all things that in them are."

(Mormon 9:7–11)

WHAT IF THE PERSON WHO IS BLESSED DIES ANYWAY?

"And it shall come to pass that those that die in me shall not taste of death, for it shall be sweet unto them. . . .

"And again, it shall come to pass that he that hath faith in me to be healed, and is not appointed unto death, shall be healed."

(Doctrine and Covenants 42:46, 48)

DOES JESUS REALLY KNOW HOW I FEEL?

"And he shall go forth, suffering pains and afflictions and temptations of every kind; and this that the word might be fulfilled which saith he will take upon him the pains and the sicknesses of his people.

"And he will take upon him death, that he may loose the bands of death which bind his people; and he will take upon him their infirmities, that his bowels may be filled with mercy, according to the flesh, that he may know according to the flesh how to succor his people according to their infirmities."

(Alma 7:11–12)

WHAT IF THE HEALING I SEEK
DOES NOT COME?

"And if thou shouldst be cast into the pit, or into the hands of murderers, and the sentence of death passed upon thee; if thou be cast into the deep; if the billowing surge conspire against thee; if fierce winds become thine enemy; if the heavens gather blackness, and all the elements combine to hedge up the way; and above all, if the very jaws of hell shall gape open the mouth wide after thee, know thou, my son, that all these things shall give thee experience, and shall be for thy good.

"The Son of Man hath descended below them all. Art thou greater than he?

"Therefore, hold on thy way, and the priesthood shall remain with thee; for their bounds are set, they cannot pass. Thy days are known, and thy years shall not be numbered less; therefore, fear not what man can do, for God shall be with you forever and ever."

(Doctrine and Covenants 122:7–9)

Endnotes

1. See Ann N. Madsen, "Medicine and Healing in the Time of Jesus," in *The Lord of the Gospels: The 1990 Sperry Symposium on the New Testament,* edited by Bruce A. Van Orden and Brent L. Top (Salt Lake City: Deseret Book, 1991), 123.

2. Boyd K. Packer, "I Will Remember Your Sins No More," *Ensign,* May 2006, 28.

3. Marion G. Romney, in Conference Report, October 1963, 25.

4. See Joseph Fielding Smith, *Essentials in Church History* (Salt Lake City: Deseret Book, 1974), 82.

5. Ivan J. Barrett, *Joseph Smith and the Restoration: A History of the Church to 1846* (Provo, Utah: BYU Press, 1973), 439–40.

6. Barrett, *Joseph Smith and the Restoration,* 440.

7. Wilford Woodruff, in *Journal of Discourses,* 26 vols. (London: Latter-day Saints' Book Depot, 1854–86), 19:225.

8. Susan Arrington Madsen, *The Lord Needed a Prophet* (Salt Lake City: Deseret Book, 1990), 82.

9. Joseph F. Smith, *Gospel Doctrine* (Salt Lake City: Deseret Book, 1975), 543.

10. Letter in the possession of the author.

11. Letter in the possession of the author.

12. Quoted by Jack Wertheimer, "Divine Intervention," in *The Wall Street Journal,* January 6, 2006, W13.

13. Joseph Smith, *History of the Church of Jesus Christ of Latter-day Saints,* edited by B. H. Roberts, 2d ed. rev., 7 vols. (Salt Lake City: The Church of Jesus Christ of Latter-day Saints: 1932–51), 2:381.

14. Harold B. Lee, *The Teachings of Harold B. Lee,* edited by Clyde J. Williams (Salt Lake City: Bookcraft, 1996), 414–15; italics in original.

15. "There Is a Balm in Gilead," traditional African-American spiritual.

16. "Come, Ye Disconsolate," *Hymns of The Church of Jesus Christ of Latter-day Saints* (Salt Lake City: The Church of Jesus Christ of Latter-day Saints, 1985), no. 115.

17. Thomas S. Monson, "Meeting Life's Challenges," *Ensign,* November 1993, 70.

18. Rachel Naomi Remen, *My Grandfather's Blessings: Stories of Strength, Refuge, and Belonging* (New York: Riverhead, 2000), 110.

19. C. S. Lewis, *Mere Christianity* (New York: HarperCollins, 2001), 202.

20. Ezra Taft Benson, "Beware of Pride," *Ensign,* May 1989, 6.

21. Gordon B. Hinckley, "The Healing Power of Christ," *Ensign,* November 1988, 54.

22. Henry B. Eyring, "In the Strength of the Lord," *Ensign,* May 2004, 17.

23. Richard G. Scott, "Peace of Conscience and Peace of Mind," *Ensign,* November 2004, 15.

24. Louisa May Alcott, *Little Women* (New York: Signet Classic, 1983), 381.

25. Victor Hugo, quoted in Richard L. Evans, *Richard Evans Quote Book* (Salt Lake City: Publishers Press, 1971), 139.

26. Ezra Taft Benson, "A Mighty Change of Heart," *Ensign,* October 1989, 5.

27. Gordon B. Hinckley, *Discourses of President Gordon B. Hinckley, Volume 2: 2000–2004* (Salt Lake City: Deseret Book, 2005), 452.

28. Hinckley, *Discourses of President Gordon B. Hinckley, Volume 2,* 189.

29. Bruce R. McConkie, *Doctrinal New Testament Commentary,* 3 vols. (Salt Lake City: Bookcraft, 1965–73), 1:188.

30. Jeffrey R. Holland, "For Times of Trouble," *BYU Devotional and Fireside Addresses* (Provo, Utah: Brigham Young University Press, 1980), 45.

31. James E. Faust, "Power of the Priesthood," *Ensign,* May 1997, 42–43.

32. James E. Talmage, *Jesus the Christ* (Salt Lake City: Deseret Book, 1983), 296.

33. "How Gentle God's Commands," *Hymns,* no. 125.

34. Robert D. Hales, "Healing Soul and Body," *Ensign,* November 1998, 15.

35. Thomas S. Monson, "Choose You This Day," *Ensign,* November 2004, 68.

36. "Lord, I Would Follow Thee," *Hymns,* no. 220.

37. George Blair, "The Carpenter of Nazareth," as quoted by Jeffery R. Holland, in "Broken Things to Mend," *Ensign,* May 2006, 71.

38. Hales, "Healing Soul and Body," 16–17.

39. Orson F. Whitney, quoted in Spencer W. Kimball, *Faith Precedes the Miracle* (Salt Lake City: Deseret Book, 1972), 98.

40. We are indebted for these insights to Maurine Jensen Proctor and Scot Facer Proctor, *Source of the Light: A Witness and Testimony of Jesus Christ, the Savior and Redeemer of the World* (Salt Lake City: Deseret Book, 1992).